THE LOGIC OF
SCIENCE IN
SOCIOLOGY

Walter Wallace

NORTHWESTERN UNIVERSITY

THE LOGIC OF SCIENCE IN SOCIOLOGY

Aldine · Atherton

CHICAGO & NEW YORK

First published 1971 by
Aldine · Atherton, Inc.
529 South Wabash Avenue
Chicago, Illinois 60605

Library of Congress Catalog Number 71-149845
ISBN 202-30193 -1, cloth; 202-30194,-x, paper
Printed in the United States of America

Second Printing   1972

ACKNOWLEDGMENTS

The author wishes to thank the following publishers for permission to quote
from their books.

The Chandler Publishing Company, an Intext Publisher for use of quotes
from THE CONDUCT OF INQUIRY by Abraham Kaplan.

Basic Books, Inc. and the Hutchinson Publishing Group for quotes from
THE LOGIC OF SCIENTIFIC DISCOVERY by Karl R. Popper (© 1959
by Karl Raimund Popper, Basic Books, Inc., Publishers, New York).

The University of Chicago Press for quotes from THE STRUCTURE OF
SCIENTIFIC REVOLUTION by Thomas Kuhn (1962).

Harcourt Brace Jovanovich, Inc. for quotes from THE STRUCTURE OF
SCIENCE by Ernest Nagel, © 1961 by Harcourt Brace Jovanovich, Inc.

Cambridge University Press for quotes from SCIENTIFIC EXPLANATION
by Richard B. Braithwaite.

PREFACE

The subject of this book is limited to the abstract form or "logic" of science (as applied particularly to scientific sociology). Therefore, neither the substantive content nor the social, economic, political, ethical, aesthetic, historical, and other causes, conditions, and consequences of any particular science, or of science as a whole, will be discussed here. My chief aim has been to compress, to simplify, and to organize into an easily understood and reasonably well-documented scheme some principal answers to questions such as: What makes a discipline "scientific" in the first place? What are theories, empirical generalizations, hypotheses, and observations; and how are they related to each other? What is meant by "the scientific method?" What roles do induction and deduction play in science? What are the places of measurement, sampling techniques, descriptive statistics, statistical inference, scale construction, tests of significance, "grand" theories, and "middle-range" theories? What parts are played by our ideas concerning logic, causality, and chance? What is the significance of the rule of parsimony? How do verbal and mathematical languages compare in expressing scientific statements?

The intended use of this book goes beyond these abstract questions, however. The discussion presented here may also serve a practical role in the sociology and history of science by providing a framework for reducing the enormous variety of scientific researches — both within a given field and across all fields — to a limited number of interrelated formal elements. Such a framework, it is hoped, may prove useful in assessing empirical relationships between the formal aspects of scientific work and its substantive, social, economic, political, and historic aspects.

Finally, I hope this book will be of use in constructing individual scientific researches. In this sense, it may be treated as a guide to consideration of the most general formal problems that seem intrinsic to all such researches.

For helping to make this book possible, I offer my thanks to Russell Sage Foundation and my colleagues there, whose support, intellectual stimulation, and books were the essential background and raw materials; to Alexander J. Morin, who always provides excellent criticism and ideas; to Richard J. Hill, who led me profitably to reconsider some problems discussed here; to Robert K. Merton, who commented encouragingly on an earlier draft of this book; and to Bern Fasse, who expertly typed my handwritten conglomerate.

Contents

Chapter One

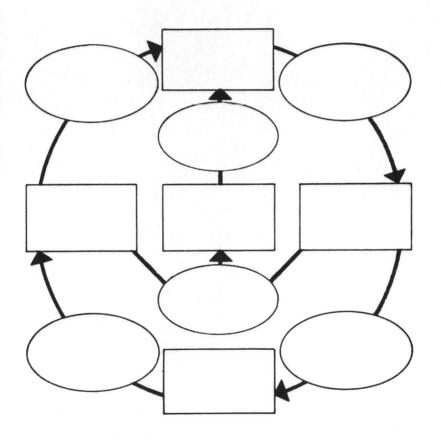

Introduction

Science and Three Alternatives

Whatever else it may be, science is a way of generating and testing the truth of statements about events in the world of human experience. But since science is only one of several ways of doing this, it seems appropriate to begin by identifying them all, specifying some of the most general differences among them, and thus locating science within the context they provide.

There are at least four ways of generating, and testing the truth of, empirical statements: "authoritarian," "mystical," "logico-rational" and "scientific."[1] A principal distinction among these is the manner in which each vests confidence in the *producer* of the statement that is alleged to be true (that is, one asks, *Who* says so?); in the *procedure* by which the statement was produced (that is, one asks, *How* do you know?): and in the *effect* of the statement (that is, one asks, What *difference* does it make?).

In the authoritarian mode, knowledge is sought and tested by referring to those who are socially defined as qualified producers of knowledge (for example, oracles, elders, archbishops,

1. The outlines of the following discussion were suggested by Montague (1925).

11

kings, presidents, professors). Here the knowledge-seeker attributes the ability to produce true statements to the natural or supernatural occupant of a particular social position. The procedure whereby the seeker solicits this authority (prayer, petition, etiquette, ceremony) is likely to be important to the nature of the authority's response, but not to the seeker's confidence in that response. Moreover, although the practical effects of the knowledge thus obtained can contribute to the eventual overthrow of authority, a very large number of effective disconfirmations may be required before this happens.

The mystical mode (including its drug- or stress-induced hallucinatory variety) is partly related to the authoritarian, insofar as both may solicit knowledge from prophets, mediums, divines, gods, and other supernaturally knowledgeable authorities. But the authoritarian mode depends essentially on the social position of the knowledge-producer, while the mystical mode depends more essentially on manifestations of the knowledge-consumer's personal "state of grace," and on his personal psychophysical state. For this reason, in the mystical mode far more may depend on applying ritualistic purification and sensitizing procedures to the consumer. This mode also extends its solicitations for knowledge beyond animistic gods, to more impersonal, abstract, unpredictably inspirational, and magical sources, such as manifest themselves in readings of the tarot, entrails, hexagrams, and horoscopes. Again, as in the case of the authoritarian mode, a very large number of effective disconfirmations may be needed before confidence in the mystical grounds for knowledge can be shaken.

In the logico-rational mode, judgment of statements purporting to be true rests chiefly on the procedure whereby these statements have been produced; and the procedure centers on the rules of formal logic. This mode is related to the authoritarian and mystical ones, insofar as the latter two can provide grounds for accepting both the rules of procedure and the axioms or "first principles" of the former. But once these grounds are accepted, for whatever reasons, strict adherence to correct procedure is held infallibly to produce valid knowledge. As in the two preceding modes, disconfirmation by effect may have little impact on the acceptability of the logico-rational mode of acquiring knowledge.

Finally, among these four modes of generating and testing empirical statements, the scientific mode combines a primary reliance on the observational effects of the statements in question, with a secondary reliance on the procedures (methods) used to generate them.[2] Relatively little weight is placed on characteristics of the producer *per se;* but when they are involved, achieved rather than ascribed characteristics are stressed — not for their own sakes, but as *prima facie* certifications of effect and procedure claims.

In emphasizing the role of methods in the scientific mode, I mean to suggest that whenever two or more items of information (for example, observations, empirical generalizations, theories) are believed to be rivals for truth-value, the choice depends heavily on a collective assessment and replication of the procedures that yielded the items.[3] In fact, all of the methods of science may be thought of as relatively strict cultural conventions whereby the production, transformation, and therefore the criticism, of proposed items of knowledge may be carried out collectively and with relatively unequivocal results. This centrality of highly conventionalized criticism seems to be what is meant when *method*[4] is sometimes said to be the essential

2. For a classic discussion of some sociological relations between the mystical, scientific, and authoritarian modes, see Malinowski (1948); and for classic experiments, essentially comparing the authoritarian and the scientific modes (that is, group influence on individual perception), see Asch (1958) and Sherif (1958). Betsy Barley (private communication) recalls Groucho's summary line in *Duck Soup:* "Who are you going to believe — me or your eyes?"

3. To say this is a distinguishing tendency of the scientific mode is not to say that this tendency is never opposed. Political pressure has been brought to bear, at various times and places, on the ideas of Galileo, Marx, Darwin, and many others.

4. My use of "method" probably incorporates some of what Nagel calls

quality of science; and it is the relative clarity and universality of this method and its several parts that make it possible for scientists to communicate across, as well as within, disciplinary lines.

Scientific methods deliberately and systematically seek to annihilate the individual scientist's standpoint. We would like to be able to say of every statement of scientific information (whether observation, empirical generalization, theory, hypothesis, or decision to accept or reject an hypothesis) that it represents an *unbiased* image of the world — not a given scientist's *personal* image of the world, and ultimately not even a *human* image of the world, but a *universal* image representing the way the world "really" is, without regard to time or place of the observed events and without regard to any distinguishing characteristics of the observer. Obviously, such disembodied "objectivity" is impossible to finite beings, and our nearest approximation to it can only be *agreement* among individual scientists. Scientific methods constitute the rules whereby agreement about specific images of the world is reached. The methodological controls of the scientific process thus annihilate the individual's standpoint, not by an impossible effort to substitute objectivity in its literal sense, but by substituting rules for intersubjective criticism, debate, and, ultimately, agreement.[5] The rules for constructing scales, drawing samples, taking measurements, estimating parameters, logically inducing and deducing, etc., become the primary bases for criticizing, rejecting, and accepting items of scientific information. Thus, ideally, criticism is not directed first to what an item of information says about the world, but to the method by which the item was produced.

But I have stressed that reliance on the *observational effects*

"technique," since he restricts scientific method to "the general logic employed . . . for assessing the merits of an inquiry" (1967:9).

5. See Nagel (1967:10).

of statements purporting to be true is even more crucial to science than is its reliance on methodological conventions. By this I mean that if, after the methodological criticism mentioned above, two information components are still believed to be rivals, the extent to which each is accepted by the scientific community tends to depend heavily on its resistance to repeated attempts to refute it by observations. Similarly, when two methodological procedures are believed to be rivals, the choice between them tends to rest on their relative abilities to generate, systematize, and predict new observations. Thus, Popper says: "I shall certainly admit a system as empirical or scientific only if it is capable of being tested by experience. . . . It must be possible for an empirical scientific system to be refuted by experience" (1961:40-41)

Assuming that observation is partly independent of the observer (that is, assuming that he can observe something other than himself, even though the observation is shaped to greater or lesser degree by that self — assuming, in short, that observations refer, partly, to something "out there," external to any observer), it becomes apparent that reliance on observation seeks the same goal as reliance on method: the annihilation of individual bias and the achievement of a "universal" image of the way the world "really" is. But there is an important difference in the manner in which the two seek this goal. Reliance on method attacks individual bias by subjecting it to highly conventionalized criticism and subordinating it to collective agreement. It thus seeks to overpower personal bias with shared bias. Reliance on observation (given the "independence" assumption mentioned above), however, introduces into both biases an element whose ultimate source is independent of all human biases, whether individual and unique or collective and shared. In a word, it seeks to temper shared bias, as well as individual bias, with *un-bias*.

Therefore, the scientific mode of generating and testing statements about the world of human experience seems to rest on

dual appeals to rules (methods) whose origin is human conven-
tion, and to events (observables) whose origin is partly nonhu-
man and nonconventional. From these two bases, science
strikes forcibly at the individual biases of its own practitioners
that they may jointly pursue, with whatever falter and doom,
a literally superhuman view of the world of human experience.

Finally, in this brief comparison of modes of generating and
testing knowledge, one should remember that neither the scientific, nor the authoritarian, nor the mystical, nor the logico-
rational mode excludes any of the others. Indeed, a typical
effort will involve some scientific observation and method, some
authoritarian footnoting and documentation, some invocations
of ritually purified (that is, trained) imagination and insight,
and some logico-rational induction and deduction; only relative
emphasis or predominance among these modes permits classifying actual cases. It is perhaps just as well so, since none of the
modes can be guaranteed, in the long run, to produce any more,
or any more accurate, or any more important, knowledge than
another. And even in the short run, a particular objective truth
discovered by mystical, authoritarian, or logico-rational (or,
indeed, random) means is no less true than the same truth
discovered by scientific means. Only our confidence in its truth
will vary, depending on which means we have been socialized
to accept with least question.

Given this initial perspective on science as compared to other
ways of testing the truth of statements about the world of
human experience, a more focused approach to it can be made.

Overview of Elements
in the Scientific Process

The scientific process may be described as involving five
principal information components whose transformations into
one another are controlled by six principal sets of methods, in

the general manner shown in Figure 1. This figure is intended to be a concise but accurate map of most of the discussion in this book; for this reason, parts of it will be reproduced at appropriate points. However, the reader may wish to turn back to the complete figure occasionally in order to keep clearly in mind its full perspective. In brief translation, Figure 1 indicates the following ideas:

Individual observations are highly specific and essentially unique items of information whose synthesis into the more general form denoted by empirical generalizations is accomplished by measurement, sample summarization, and parameter estimation. Empirical generalizations, in turn, are items of information that can be synthesized into a theory via concept formation, proposition formation, and proposition arrangement. A theory, the most general type of information, is transformable into new hypotheses through the method of logical deduction. An empirical hypothesis is an information item that becomes transformed into new observations via interpretation of the hypothesis into observables, instrumentation, scaling, and sampling. These new observations are transformable into new empirical generalizations (again, via measurement, sample summarization, and parameter estimation), and the hypothesis that occasioned their construction may then be tested for conformity to them. Such tests may result in a new informational outcome: namely, a decision to accept or reject the truth of the tested hypothesis. Finally, it is inferred that the latter gives confirmation, modification, or rejection of the theory.[6]

Before going any further in detailing the meaning of Figure 1 and of the translation above, I must emphasize that the processes described there and throughout this book occur (1) some-

6. Compare Bergmann's similar, but more abbreviated, formula: "The three pillars on which the house of science is built are observation, induction, and deduction" (1957:31). For other capsule descriptions of the scientific process, see Popper (1961:111), Bohm (1961:4,5), Kaplan (1964:9-10), Stinchcombe (1968:15-18), Blalock (1969:8), and Greer (1969:4).

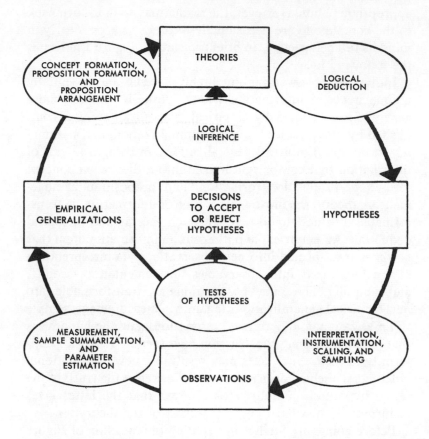

Note: Informational components are shown in rectangles; methodological controls are shown in ovals; information transformations are shown by arrows.

Figure 1. The Principal Informational Components, Methodological Controls, and Information Transformations of the Scientific Process.

times quickly, sometimes slowly; (2) sometimes with a very high degree of formalization and rigor, sometimes quite informally, unself-consciously, and intuitively; (3) sometimes through the interaction of several scientists in distinct roles (of, say, "theorist," "research director," "interviewer," "methodologist," "sampling expert," "statistician," etc.), sometimes through the efforts of a single scientist; and (4) sometimes only in the scientist's imagination, sometimes in actual fact. In other words, although Figure 1 and the discussion in this book are intended to be *systematic* renderings of science as a field of socially organized human endeavor, they are not intended to be inflexible. The task I have chosen is to set forth the principal common elements — the themes — on which a very large number of variations can be, and are, developed by different scientists. It is not my principal aim here to analyze these many possible and actual variations; I wish only to state their underlying themes. Still, it seems useful to discuss briefly the types of variation mentioned above (particularly the last type), if only to defend the claim that my analysis of themes is flexible enough to incorporate, by implication, the analysis of variations as well.

Each scientific subprocess (for example, that of transforming one information component into another, and that of applying a given methodological control) almost always involves a series of preliminary *trials*. Sometimes these trials are wholly imaginary; that is, the scientist manipulates images in his mind of objects not present to his senses. He may think, "If I had this sort of instrument, then these observations might be obtained; these generalizations and this theory and this hypotheses might be generated; etc."; or perhaps, "If I had a different theory, then I might entertain a different hypothesis — one that would conform better to existing empirical generalizations." When these imaginary trials, sometimes running several times through the entire sequence of scientific transformations, seem to be accomplished all in one instant (and when, of course, these imaginary trials turn out, when actualized, to be correct and fruitful), the scientist's performance is said to be "insightful." It is here, in making imaginary trials, that "intuition," "intelligent speculation," and "heuristic devices" find their special usefulness in science.

For maximum social acceptance as statements of truth by the scientific community, trials must not be left to imagination alone; they must become actual fact. The actualization of scientific processes (for example, actually constructing a desired instrument) usually brings about a reduction in speed and an increase in the rigor and formalization with which trials are carried out, because it subjects the entire trial process to the constraints and intransigences of the material world. An increase in the role specialization of the scientists who carry out the trials is also likely to result.

It is important to note that in the trial process just referred to (whether imaginary or actualized), directions of influence opposite to those shown in Figure 1 are often taken temporarily.[7] For example, the first formulation of a hypothesis deduced from a theory may be ambiguous, imprecise, logically faulty, untestable, or otherwise unsatisfactory, and it may undergo several revisions before a satisfactory formulation is constructed. In this process, not only will the deduced hypothesis change, but the originating theory may also be modified as the implications of each trial formulation reveal more about the theory itself.

Similarly (to move further around Figure 1), the process of transforming a hypothesis into observations may involve several interpretation trials, several scaling trials (in which new scales may be invented and alternative scales selected), and several sampling trials. In each trial (at this point in the scientific process, trials are often called "pretests" or "pilot studies"), new observations are at least imagined and often

7. I am indebted to Richard J. Hill for pointing this out to me; the "temporarily" and the "trial" ideas are my own interpretations, however.

actually made; and from them the investigator judges not only how relevant to his hypothesis the final observations and empirical generalizations are likely to be, but how appropriate his hypothesis is, given the observations and generalizations he can make. He may also judge how appropriate his methods are, given the information he is seeking to transform. Thus, the invention and trial of a new scaling, or instrumentation, or sampling, or interpretation technique may result in the deduction of new hypotheses rather than the reverse process shown in Figure 1.

Despite these retrograde effects that may be seen for every information transformation indicated in Figure 1, the dominant processual directions remain as shown there. When counterdirections are taken, they are best described as background preparations and repairs prior to a new advance. Thus, the invention of a new instrument for taking observations may occasion the deduction of new hypotheses, so that when new observations are actually and formally taken with the new instrument, they will be scientifically interpretable (that is, transformable into empirical generalizations that will be comparable with hypotheses, etc.) rather than mere extra-scientific curiosities. Similarly, a particular formulation of a theoretically-deduced hypothesis may react on its parent theory or on the method of logical deduction, and the theory may react on its supporting empirical generalizations, decisions, and on the rules of logical induction; so that when the next step is actually taken (that is, when observations are made, via interpretation of the hypothesis, scaling, instrumentation, and sampling), it will rest on newly-examined and firm ground.

But as C. Wright Mills implied, such careful background preparation does not always occur, and in practice any element in the scientific process may vary widely in the degree of its formalization and integration with other elements. Mills argued specifically that the relationship of theorizing to other phases in the scientific process can be so tenuous that theory becomes distorted and enslaved by "the fetishism of the Concept." Similarly, he claimed, the relationship of research methods to hypotheses, observations, and empirical generalizations can be so rigid that empirical research becomes distorted by "the methodological inhibition."[8] It may be added that the distinction between researches that "explore" given phenomena and researches that "test" specific hypotheses is another manifestation of the same variability in degree of formalization and integration; "exploratory" studies, precisely because they probe new substantive or methodological areas, may rest on still unformalized and unintegrated theoretical, hypothetical, and methodological arguments. Understanding a published report of such a study often depends on inferring the theory that "must have" undergirded the study, or on guessing the empirical generalizations, or hypotheses, or observations, or tests, etc., that the researcher "must have" had in mind. "Hypothesis-testing" studies, however, are likely to have more explicit, more formalized, and more thoroughly integrated foundations in all elements of the scientific process.[9]

Finally, in this preliminary description of elements in the scientific process, it seems useful to note that sociologists (and other scientists, as well) often refer simply to "theory" (or "theory construction") and "empirical research" as the two major constituents of science. What is the relation of these familiar terms to the more detailed elements just outlined?

8. Mills dubbed these two distortions "grand theory" and "abstracted empiricism" (1959:25-75). Glaser and Strauss also derisively contrast "logico-deductive theory, which . . . was merely thought up on the basis of *a priori* assumption and a touch of common sense, peppered with a few old theoretical speculations made by the erudite," with "grounded" theory — theory generated "from data systematically obtained from social research" (1967:29,2).

9. Diana Crane (in press) suggests that exploratory studies, and the variant of the scientific process that they represent, are typical of an early stage of growth in a scientific discipline (Kuhn's "preparadigm" period, 1964), | whereas | hypothesis-testing | studies | are typical of a more mature ("paradigm-based") stage.

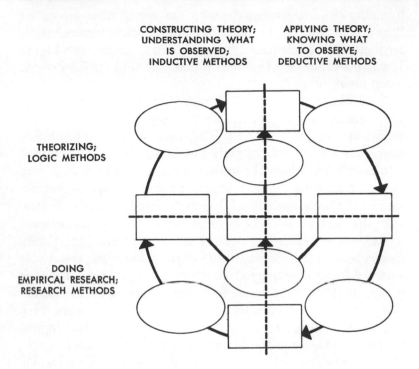

Figure 2. Classification of the Principal Components, Controls, and Transformations of the Scientific Process According to Some Conventional Terms.

Figure 2 is designed to answer this question by suggesting that the left half of Figure 1 represents what seems to be meant by the inductive construction of theory from, and understanding of, observations; whereas the right half represents what seems to be meant by the deductive application of theory to observations and the knowledge of observations.[10] Similarly, the top half of Figure 1 represents what is often referred to as theorizing, via the use of inductive and deductive logic as method; whereas the bottom half represents what is often meant

10. I use "application" in its scientific, rather in its engineering, sense.

by doing empirical research, with the aid of what are called "research methods." The manifold interrelations between these segments of the scientific process should be clear from Figure 1, which also suggests that the process may be as readily divided along many other lines.[11]

It will be noted in Figure 2, however, that all five information components, and two of the methodological control sets, are shown in marginal positions. The marginality of information components is meant to signify their ability to be transformed into each other, under the indicated controls, and thus to play at least dual roles in the scientific process. Of special importance is the transformational line up the middle. This line represents the closely related claims that tests of congruence between hypotheses and empirical generalizations depend on the deductive as well as the inductive side of scientific work and are as essential to constructing as to applying theory; that decisions to accept or reject hypotheses form an indispensable bridge between constructing and applying theory and also between theorizing and doing empirical research; and that the logical inference controlling the incorporation of such decisions into theory is marginal between constructing and applying theory. By pointing out these marginalities, I mean to emphasize the paramount importance of this series of methodological controls and information components, wherein "concrete" observations made on the world and "abstract" theories made within the

11. For a more detailed discussion of some interdependencies based on the "theory-versus-research" distinction, see Robert K. Merton, "The Bearing of Sociological Theory on Empirical Research," and "The Bearing of Empirical Research on Sociological Theory" (1957:85-117). Figure 1 also embraces the factors that Kuhn indicates are meant by his term "paradigm." Kuhn says: "By choosing [the term] paradigm I mean to suggest that some accepted examples of actual scientific practise — examples which include law, theory, application, and instrumentation together — provide models from which spring particular coherent traditions of scientific research" (1964:10); although at one point (1964:77) Kuhn identifies "theory" alone with "paradigm."

mind are brought together in their most intimate confrontation, with inevitably profound consequences for both.

An Illustration Based on Durkheim's *Suicide*

The formulations presented so far are relatively abstract. An illustration based on Durkheim's famous study (first released in 1897) may convey the overall sense of the process which the rest of this book dissects for closer examination. (It must be emphasized that in this illustration I am not concerned with how empirically true my statements about suicide are, nor am I much concerned with how accurately they reproduce Durkheim's statements; instead, I am concerned chiefly that the form of my statements illustrates Figure 1, and thus illustrates how scientific statements about suicide *would* be generated and their truth tested.)[12]

Suppose a scientist became interested in explaining why suicide rates are higher among some people than others. Such an interest is almost certain to be generated by prior theory and hypotheses (Durkheim indicated in the Preface to *Suicide,* pages 35-39, that his own interest was so generated), even though they may be vague, implicit, and unconsciously held. But the first explicit step in satisfying one's research interest would be to interpret the concept "suicide" in terms of phenomena on which observations can actually be made.[13]

Following that, one might choose or construct the scales that

12. For his statements, see Durkheim, *Suicide* (1951); and for summaries of the present state of knowledge about suicide, see Gibbs (1966 and 1968), and Douglas (1967).

13. For his part, Durkheim interpreted suicide as "cases of death resulting directly or indirectly from a positive or negative act of the victim himself, which he knows will produce this result" (1951:44). The extent to which this is an interpretation that refers to phenomena that were in actual nineteenth century practise *observable* (particularly considering the last clause of Durkheim's interpretation) is, of course, questionable.

are to be applied to these observations. Durkheim used the ratio scale of counting; the nominal scales of religious affiliation, sex, nationality, etc.; the interval scale of calendar year; and the (obviously) ordinal scale of marital status.

Next, the instruments whereby observations will be made are determined. Durkheim relied on official documents (which he accepted as accurately recording observations on suicide as he interpreted the term) and the published works of others.

Then, decisions regarding sampling procedures are made. Durkheim sampled suicides presumably committed during given years of the nineteenth century, in various geopolitical units of Europe, by persons in given age categories, by persons of given sex, etc.

Finally, by acting in accord with the above methodological decisions, a large number of individual observations would be collected. These observations would be measured by the appropriate scales and the measures would then be summarized in the form of rates, averages, totals, maps, tables, graphs, and the like. Since these summaries would refer only to the observations that were actually in the samples, some estimate would be made of the corresponding true (that is, error-free) values of these measures in the populations from which the samples were drawn. Durkheim does not seem to have considered this question explicitly, and simply treated his sample statistics as if they were population parameters.

At this point, the large number of observations so laboriously collected might be reduced to a brief but informationally heavy-laden empirical generalization: "suicide varies with Catholic and Protestant religious affiliation."

The next information transformation (of empirical generalization into theory) involves four entirely mental steps: (1) forming a concept (explanans) that identifies some characteristic that the examined religious affiliation populations, together with other populations still unexamined, may have in different degree, and that may logically or causally account for their having different suicide rates; (2) forming a concept (explanandum) that identifies some characteristic that suicide rates have in common with other conceivable rates, by virtue of which they might all be logical or causal consequences of the explanans; (3) forming a proposition in which the explanans and explanandum are related in a way consistent with the relationship stated in the originating empirical generalization; and (4) forming several such propositions, all sharing a common explanandum or a common explanans, and arranging them in such a way that further hypotheses can be deduced and tested.

To continue the Durkheim-based example, the first step (forming the explanans) means that one might arrive at a statement such as, "Suicide rates vary inversely with the *social integration of individuals* in its very-low-to-moderate range." Here only religious affiliation — the independent variable of the originating empirical generalization — has been theoretically conceptualized. After the second step, one might say, "The *incidence of deviant behavior* varies inversely with the social integration of individuals in its very-low-to-moderate range," thus adding a more abstract conceptualization of suicide rate[14] — the original dependent variable. The third step might yield a theoretic proposition of the following kind: "The social integration of individuals, in its very-low-to-moderate range, causes, in inverse ratio, the incidence of deviant behavior." Here the explanans and explanandum are related as cause and effect — a relationship consistent with that in the original empirical generalization, but going beyond observable "covariation" to the more abstract "causation."[15]

Finally, in the fourth step, through reiterations of the above process (beginning with the transformation of observations into

14. In the main body of *Suicide,* Durkheim did not conceptualize suicide rate at any higher level of abstraction, and for this reason, his theory remains somewhat asymmetrical. In the Preface to *Suicide,* however, he did suggest that high suicide rates were symptomatic of "the general contemporary maladjustment being undergone by European societies" (1951:37).
15. See Blalock (1968:155).

empirical generalizations) one might develop three other Durk-heim-like propositions. Then, all four propositions (together with necessary definitions) might be arranged into the following concatenated theory:

Definitions:

(1) "Deviant behavior" refers to individuals' violations of particular behavioral prescriptions or proscriptions promulgated by others.

(2) "Social integration" refers to the degree to which individuals objectively receive benefits and injuries provided by others, and so are integrated into the latter's social system.

(3) "Normative integration" refers to the degree to which individuals subjectively accept behavioral prescriptions and proscriptions promulgated by others, and so are integrated into the latter's normative system.

Propositions:

The incidence of deviant behavior is caused:

(1) In inverse ratio by social integration in its very-low-to-moderate (egoism) range;

(2) In direct ratio by social integration in its moderate-to-very-high (altruism) range;

(3) In inverse ratio by normative integration in its very-low-to-moderate (anomie) range; and

(4) In direct ratio by normative integration in its moderate-to-very-high (fatalism) range.

From such a theory, one could deduce, interpret, and finally test new hypotheses purporting to explain the incidence of kinds of deviant behavior other than suicide by referring to manifestations of social and normative integration other than those actually examined in the process of generating the theory. For example (again drawn from Durkheim), if it could be shown that unmarried persons experience less social integration than married persons, and that both are in the very-low-to-moderate range of social integration, then the theory predicts that the unmarried will have a higher suicide rate, and a higher incidence of other deviant behavior, than the married. New observations and new empirical generalizations to test the truth of this new hypothesis could be generated as before, by interpreting the hypothesis into directly observable terms, scaling, instrumentation, and sampling; and by measurement, summarization, and parameter estimation. Then the new empirical generalizations could be compared with the hypothesis; and if the comparison were judged favorable, a decision to accept the hypothesis would be made and confirmation for the theory would be inferred (or, more precisely, no disconfirmation would be inferred). If the theory were to remain unchanged, results of tests of many such hypotheses would describe the limits of the theory. That is, such results would indicate which varieties of "deviant behavior," "social integration," and "normative integration" fall within its explanatory scope, and which varieties do not. But since scientists are usually more interested in expanding than in describing the limits of a theory, it would almost certainly be modified under the impact of each test that did not give positive results.

Against the background of all the foregoing comments, and particularly this illustration based on Durkheim, let us approach each element of Figure 1 more closely. I have already noted the pivotal role of empirical observation in the scientific mode of acquiring knowledge; for this reason my discussion begins with this information component, and then moves clockwise around Figure 1. One could begin with any other component or control or transformation, however, since the process indicated by Figure 1 has no actual beginning or end but only didactically convenient or inconvenient ones.

Chapter Two

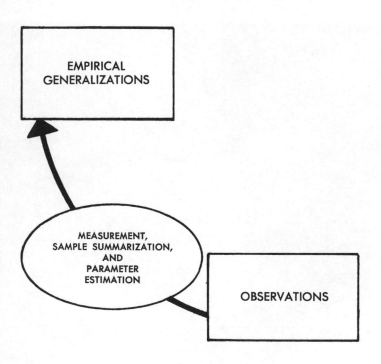

EMPIRICAL
GENERALIZATIONS

MEASUREMENT,
SAMPLE SUMMARIZATION,
AND
PARAMETER
ESTIMATION

OBSERVATIONS

Observations;
Measurement, Sample Summarization,
and Parameter Estimation;
Empirical Generalizations

Observations

Observations seem to be so nearly the prime arbiters of the entire scientific process that Nagel argues:

> Scientific thought takes its ultimate point of departure from problems suggested by observing things and events encountered in common experience; it aims to understand these observable things by discovering some systematic order in them; and its final test for the laws that serve as instruments of explanation and prediction is their concordance with such observations (1961:79).[1]

But the primacy of observations in science should not be taken to mean that observations are "immediately given" or wholly detached in their origins from the empirical generalizations, theories, and hypotheses to which they then give rise. On the contrary, the very procedures whereby observations are made seem to depend partly on the prior existence of other informational components of the scientific process; Ourobouros forever feeds on, and generates, its own tail.

Popper, for example, says:

> The naive empiricist . . . thinks that we begin by collecting and

1. See also Braithwaite (1960:255).

arranging our experiences, and so ascend the ladder of science. . .
But if I am ordered: "Record what you are now experiencing" I
shall hardly know how to obey this ambiguous order. Am I to
report that I am writing; that I hear a bell ringing; a newsboy
shouting; a loudspeaker droning; or am I to report, perhaps, that
these noises irritate me? . . . A science needs points of view, and
theoretical problems (1961:106).

And Wartofsky argues that:

Any descriptive utterance, any observation statement is already a
hypothesis; and further, . . . every such hypothesis already carries
with it a matrix of relevance which guides us to engage in those tests
of experience which we take to support or to fail to support this
hypothesis (1968:182).[2]

If ordinary, everyday observation is thus dependent on prior
information components (for example, hypothesis) and
methodological controls (for example, tests), how much more
so is scientific observation, whose most distinguishing mark is
the deliberate control exercised over it. As Kaplan puts the
matter, every observation in science is:

First of all something done, an act performed by the scientist. . .
Scientific observation is deliberate search, carried out with care and
forethought, as contrasted with the casual and largely passive per-
ceptions of everyday life. It is this deliberateness and control of the
process of observation that is distinctive of science, not merely the
use of special instruments (important as they are) — save as this use
is itself indicative of forethought and care. . . . Above all, "observation" means that special care is being taken: the root meaning of
the word is not just "to see", but "to watch over" (Kaplan 1964:
126–127).[3]

2. See also Hanson (1967).
3. It may be noted, in passing, that Kaplan's emphasis here on deliberate
control as a pivotal distinction between scientific and everyday observation
seems to relate to the difference between what he calls "knowing something
and having an experience of it." Kaplan says, "It is one thing to know that
the day is warm, and another to feel its warmth. Though the cognitive process

But to say that scientific observations are dependent on other elements in the scientific process does not preclude saying that they are also partly independent of them. Indeed, the same must be said of every information component, every methodological control, and every information transformation shown in Figure 1; none is *wholly* dependent on the others. Thus, the system depicted in Figure 1 is not, in actual fact, a closed system at any point; inputs to it are omitted from that diagram, and are merely mentioned in this book, solely for reasons of analytical focus. But note that I have already made such mention of the social structure of scientific institutions, and of the societal structure that environs them, as input sources. And the other ideational subsystems of culture — that is, the aesthetic and ethical ones — make their inputs to the scientific process when the "beauty" or "elegance" or the "moral justification" of a proposed informational component, methodological control, or information transformation becomes a consideration. Still other sources of possible inputs to the scientific process should be noted (for example, the number, and recruitment and expulsion rates of scientists at a given moment in the history of science; their distribution in space and time with reference especially to scientific resources; their inherited and acquired psychological and physiological characteristics; and the prevailing level of general technological capacity in the society as a whole and in science particularly).

Finally (especially in the present context of the role of observations in the scientific process), "sensing — which we may take as a basic organic activity at the level of the surface recep-

---

itself is an experience, as richly concrete as any other, *what* is known is something abstract, formulable in a proposition. . . . (and) no limited set of propositions can exhaust the content of an experience of the situation" (1964: 208). The sciences should not be misconstrued: they seek only knowledge, not the re-creation of experience. The latter pursuit falls to the arts, and to an increasing variety of chemical, hypnotic, psychoanalytic, and electrical stimulations of the brain.

tors of a percipient organism" (Wartofsky 1968:102) — must be mentioned as making its own unique and independent input in the scientific process. That is, if "the sense data are typically conceived of as qualitative impressions: color patches, shapes, tones, sensory qualities of hardness, softness, smoothness, and so on" (Wartofsky 1968:102), then it will make a difference to the scientist's ultimate observation statement if he senses, say, smoothness or roughness, a blue color patch or a red one, and so on. Moreover, if the sensory "receptors" may indeed be said to receive "impressions" impinging on them from outside, then at least some of this observation difference may be attributed to such external signals, which may in turn operate to some degree independently of the receptors. On this (admittedly, variable) degree of observer-independence would seem to rest the conclusion that "we do not simply see what we like or wish to see, nor is our observation simply a function of expectation . . . ." (Wartofsky 1968:122) and therefore the conclusion that observations constitute a genuine informational input to, and not only an output of, the scientific process.[4]

Measurement

Thus, when stressing observations as *outputs* of prior information and method, one can point out the simultaneity of observation and measurement: "All scientific observation is, to one degree or another, measurement. The simple observational statement, 'I observe that the ball is red,' already carries with it the framework within which 'ball' and 'red' are distinguishable from 'not ball' and 'not red' by some critical attributes which permit us to classify" (Wartofsky 1968:174-175). But when stressing the independent *input* character of observa-

4. The observer-independent element in observations seems acknowledged (although differently so) in phenomenalist as well as realist views. Linguistic and pragmatic views neither deny nor avow this element; it is irrelevant to their concerns. See Wartofsky (1968:108-113).

tions, one can note that observations are frequently made through some instrument (say, a camera, a voting machine, a tape recorder, a paper-and-pencil questionnaire, the observer's ear and memory of tonal pitch, etc.) and then measured — in the sense of deliberate comparison with some scale of pertinent values — afterward, in the manner suggested by Figure 1.

Partly for this reason, Figure 1 divides what is often treated as a single process ("measurement") into two phases: devising or selecting the scale employed in measurement ("scaling"), and applying this scale according to a set of procedural rules ("measurement"). Through this division, I mean to claim that scales — although they may actually be developed after the making of certain observations whose *kind* the scale is being tailored to measure (see the discussion in Chapter 1 of "trials" and retrograde directions in the scientific process) — always antedate the *particular* observations that they measure. When this point is combined with the one just made — that the measurement of observations often follows the making of observations — the conclusion may be drawn that if observations happen to be made for which no scale already exists or to which no measurement procedure can be applied, the observations need not be discarded as useless or meaningless. They may become serendipitous events leading toward new and revealing empirical generalizations, theories, etc., if they are held until adequate scaling and measurement procedures are devised for them.

In general, measurement may be defined as any procedure whereby observations are systematically assigned symbols ("scale values") among which certain specified relations are conventionally defined as legitimate. Thus, measurement procedures always consist in comparing an observation with a set of abstract symbols (such as words, numbers, letters, colors, sounds, etc.) and assigning, according to some prior rule, one or more such symbols to the observation.[5] Thereafter, since the

5. Kaplan says "the objects (to be measured) are *mapped* into an abstract

assignment rule and the repertoire of legitimate relationships between the assigned symbols has been established in advance (by the procedures of scaling, discussed in Chapter 4), the measured observation can be symbolically manipulated in any way that repertoire permits. Thus, the symbolic representation contained in measurement endows the scientist with vastly increased ability to manipulate observations, and also with relatively clear rules specifying and limiting the nature and logical consequences of these manipulations. Most observations, indeed, can *only* be compared symbolically. For example, observations on social groups that existed ten thousand years apart can only be compared through, say, comparing the numbers and names of their participants, the frequencies and names of their interactions, etc. In general, it may be said that observations themselves are liable to only a severely limited repertoire of manipulations; they cannot be added, or subtracted, or percentaged, or correlated, or introduced as subjects or objects in sentences, or employed as elements in graphs, diagrams, or pictures. Only the appropriate kinds of symbols for such observations (and for their derivatives — empirical generalizations, theories, and hypotheses) can be so manipulated.[6]

---

space of some determinate structure" (1964:177), and he quotes Weyl as saying that the only decisive feature of all measurements is "symbolic representation" (1964:178).

6. From this general superiority (for scientific purposes) that symbols have over the observations to which they are assigned seems to flow the two more specifically comparison-related "functions of measurement" that may be inferred from Kaplan's discussion: (1) Measurement permits an estimate of sameness among observations made on different "kinds" of phenomena (for example, a pound of feathers equals a pound of iron filings); and (2) measurement permits an estimate of difference among observations made on the same "kind" of phenomena (for example, one pound of feathers is not equal to one and one-tenth pound of feathers). Kaplan's own words are "Measurement, in a word, is a device . . . by which we are assured of equivalences among objects of diverse origin. . . . A second function of measurement . . . is to make possible more subtle discriminations and correspondingly more precise descriptions" (1964:173-174).

The "kinds" into which phenomena are divided at any given moment in

Sample Summarization

But the assignment of a scale value to an observation is subject to an unavoidable imprecision that imposes a classificatory generalization on all empirical observations. Popper says:

> Measurement should be described in the following terms. We find that the point of the body to be measured lies between two gradations or marks on the measuring-rod or, say, that the pointer of our measuring apparatus lies *between* two gradations on the scale. . . Thus an interval, a range, always remains (1961:125).

As a result, all observations falling within a given measurement interval, although they are all in fact different from one another, become indistinguishable according to that scale and are treated by it as if they were absolutely identical. The formation of empirical generalizations operates first, therefore, at the level of individual observations. At the level of summarizing a sample of individual observations into "averages," "rates," "scores," and the like, this process is even clearer. Here, those techniques called "descriptive statistics" find their nearly indispensable place in the scientific process. On this general question, Nagel points out that:

> In measuring the velocity of sound in a given gas, different numerical values are in general obtained when the measurement is repeated. Accordingly, if a definite numerical value is to be assigned to the velocity, these different numbers must be "averaged" in some fashion, usually in accordance with an assumed law of experimental error. In short, the law about the velocity of sound in gases does not formulate relations between the immediate data of sense (1961:82).[7]

---

the history of science are by no means fixed, and are profoundly responsive to measured estimates of similarities and differences along various dimensions. Thus, the ancient distinctions of "kind" between earth, air, water, and fire have been superceded by a succession of new "kinds" of matter, partly as a result of changed measurement scales and procedures.

7. Kaplan refers to "the fiction of the true measure," and argues that "we

It is important to re-emphasize that the generalization process is unavoidable and occurs with or without the investigator's conscious consent, by virtue not only of deliberate efforts to summarize or "reduce" sample data but also by virtue of the sensitivity limits of his measuring instruments.

Parameter Estimation

But there is at least one further step that enables the transformation of observations into empirical generalizations. Since every science seeks universal truths (statements that are expected to hold across all instances of given phenomena)[8] merely summarizing or "averaging" the scale values obtained by measuring a sample of observations is insufficient. These values may represent a biased sample of the values that might be obtained if all possible observations on the phenomena of interest were made and accurately assigned scale values. Obviously, statements based on a biased sample would lack any simple applicability to the full universe-of-interest; that is, they would lack the desired universality. Parameter estimation — whether employing the techniques of statistical inference or less rigorous, more informal procedures — therefore becomes an essential control over the transformation of observations into empirical generalizations. Through it, the scientist seeks to estimate (and demonstrate the grounds for his estimation) the range of values that could be expected in the observable universe-of-interest if the observed sample (of given size and produced by given procedures) were actually representative of it. He thereby seeks to estimate the extent to which empirical summaries that refer to this observed sample are transformable into empirical generali-

---

correct measurements, reduce their error; but we do so always only up to a point" (1964:202).

8. Wartofsky says "We require a law to state that something is unrestrictedly true for all possible instances where the number is presumably indefinitely larger than that of the observed instances . . ." (1968:250).

zations that refer to his still (and always) unobserved universe-of-interest.

Not only universality but precision is desired of empirical generalizations; and as a consequence, certain methodological controls are specified whereby the latter as well as the former can be maximized. Thus the scientist can take certain steps to narrow the range of values to be expected in the unobserved universe-of-interest (that is, in order to make a more precise estimation of parameters) — steps bearing especially on the manner in which his observable sample is drawn and the size of that sample.

Sometimes a single observation is provisionally accepted as yielding the best available parameter estimation (for example, naturally occurring forms on the Earth are still our only observations on the nature of social phenomena). This acceptance may result from prohibitive costs or other difficulties associated with making more than one observation, but in all such cases, everything depends on the representativeness of the single observation. And the validity of claims about such representativeness depends on the actual variability that is present in the universe of such observations. Should further observations become possible, and should they reveal important variability, the single observation would (or should) be immediately displaced in favor of a more accurate empirical generalization. This is the logic that underlies the scientist's wariness of individual "case studies" and his insistence on replication, for on the accuracy of empirical generalizations must rest the validity of theories that are invented to explain them and to predict other, related, empirical generalizations.

Empirical Generalizations

In any event, through applying the measurement, sample summarization, and parameter estimation procedures just mentioned, many or few individual observations are transformed into empirical generalizations. Braithwaite defines such a generalization as "a proposition asserting a universal connection between properties," and adds that:

> The generalization may assert a concomitance of properties in the same thing or event . . . . or it may assert that of every two events or things of which the first has the property A and stands in the relation R to the second, the second has the property B. . . . Or it may make more complicated but similar assertions about three or four or more things. The relationship between the things may be a relationship holding between simultaneous events in the things, or it may hold between events in the same thing or in two or more things which are not simultaneous (1960:9).

The underlying logic whereby observations are transformed into empirical generalizations (or, as Braithwaite says it, "the inference of an empirical generalization from its instances" [1960:257n.]) is often referred to as induction (see Figure 2). Braithwaite describes two types of "inductive principles":

> There are, first, principles of induction by simple enumeration according to which an inductive hypothesis is to be treated as being well established if it has not been refuted by experience and has been confirmed by not fewer than n positive instances. . . . There are, secondly, principles of elimination according to which an inductive hypothesis is taken to be well established if, while it has not been refuted by experience, alternative hypotheses have been so refuted (1960:260).

To such "enumerative induction" and "eliminative induction," Wartofsky adds that form which is most familiar to sociologists: namely, "statistical generalization."[9] He argues that "A statistical generalization makes the inductive inference that (a ratio of relative frequency of some property or some relation among properties) will continue to be observed as the total

---

9. See also Black's (1967), and Wartofsky's (1968:210-227) discussions of the justifications and critiques of induction.

number of observations continues to grow" (1968:234). But, "A condition of the validity of such (an inference) is the presumed randomness of the sample from which such generalizations are made"; and "The norms for such randomness are set forth in the ideal case in . . . the mathematical calculus of probabilities" (1968:239). In fact, one can go still further, and say that the immediate conditions of the validity of a statistical generalization include not only the measurement, sample summarization, and parameter estimation procedures yielding the generalization itself, but all of the procedures yielding the observations whose transformation the generalization represents. These include (in addition to sampling procedures) instrumentation, scaling, and interpretation procedures — as shown in Figure 1 and as discussed in Chapter 4 of this book.

Chapter Three

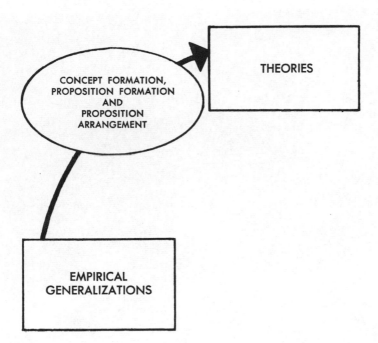

Empirical Generalizations; Concept Formation, Proposition Formation, and Proposition Arrangement; Theories

Empirical Generalizations and Theories

Merton defines an empirical generalization as "an isolated proposition summarizing observed uniformities of relationships between two or more variables" (1957:95), reserving the term "scientific law" for "a statement of invariance *derivable* from a theory" (1957:96).[1] This distinction between empirical generalizations for which appropriately explanatory theories do not yet exist and those for which such theories already exist seems important, but it is less emphasized by other writers. For example, Braithwaite maintains: "While there is general agreement that a scientific law includes a generalization, there is no agreement as to whether or not it includes anything else" (1960:10). And Nagel defines an "experimental law" simply as formula-

1. This seems to parallel another of Merton's distinctions, between serendipitous and non-serendipitous findings; a serendipitous finding is one that is not *predicted* by an available theory, whereas an empirical generalization is one that is not *explained* by an available theory (See Merton 1957:103-108). Clearly, serendipitous findings and empirical generalizations challenge the scientist to revise or reject an inadequate theory and construct a new one. Kuhn discusses the role of such challenges ("crises") in initiating scientific "revolutions" (1964). See also Kaplan's discussion of "cryptic data" as those that "not uncommonly . . . provide a point of departure for significant theoretical advance" (1964:134).

47

ting "a relation between things (or traits of things) that are observable . . ." (1961:80).

One importance of Merton's distinction is best seen in light of Zetterberg's (1963:35) distinction between a "theoretical hypothesis" (a proposition for which there is not yet empirical support) and a "theoretic invariance: law" (a proposition for which there is already empirical support). Cross-classifying the two distinctions suggests four types of statements about reality: those for which both theoretical and empirical bases are present (called "theoretic invariance" by Zetterberg, and "law" by both Merton and Zetterberg); those for which theoretical basis but no empirical basis is present (called "theoretic hypotheses" by Zetterberg); those for which empirical basis but no theoretical basis is present (called "empirical generalizations" by Merton); and those for which neither theoretical nor empirical basis is present (perhaps indicated by Kaplan's use of "fantasy" or "presuppositions" (1964:35, 86), and by some uses of the term "imagination"). In this scheme, two developmental paths may be traced from fantasy to law. In the fantasy-to-theoretic hypotheses-to-law path, one finds or constructs a theory from which the fantasy can be deduced as a novel hypothesis, tests the hypothesis, and induces the result into theory as law. In the fantasy-to-empirical generalization-to-law path, one finds or constructs a pattern of observations into which the fantasy can be induced as a novel case, and further induces the result into theory as law.

Thus, one utility of Merton's and Zetterberg's distinctions — on which this scheme rests — is that they enable us formally to differentiate two frequently contending styles whereby "ideas" (fantasy, in the above scheme) can become transformed into "understanding" (law, in the above scheme) — styles that might be characterized as "theoretically-inclined" and "empirically-inclined," respectively. Scientific development in the reverse direction (that is, from law-to-fantasy) has also occurred — as witness the demise of laws involving planetary epicycles, phlogiston, the ether, entelechy, etc — but such developments seem to have followed only one path: law-to-(disconfirmed)-theoretic hypothesis-to-fantasy.

A second and more weighty significance of Merton's distinction between those empirical generalizations that are supported by a theory and others that are not lies in its implicit recognition that being related to other empirical generalizations confers additional explanatory power on an otherwise isolated fact. As part of a theory, a given empirical generalization contributes to our understanding, not only directly of phenomena to which it specifically refers but also indirectly of phenomena not specified by it but specified by other empirical generalizations to which it is theoretically related. The reverse is also true: the other empirical generalizations to which the generalization in question is related contribute indirectly to our understanding of the phenomena to which it refers. However, it should be emphasized that empirical generalizations always retain an important degree of independence from any theoretic framework from which they are derivable. Nagel states this point as follows:

> Even when an experimental law is explained by a given theory and is thus incorporated into the framework of the latter's ideas . . . , two characteristics continue to hold for the law. It retains a meaning that can be formulated independently of the theory; and it is based on observational evidence that may enable the law to survive the eventual demise of the theory. . . . Such facts indicate that an experimental law has, so to speak, a life of its own, not contingent of the continued life of any particular theory that might explain the law" (1961:86-87).

But no matter how one conceives the relations between empirical generalizations and laws on the one hand and theories on the other, the most important point in the present discussion is the simple and agreed-upon relation of generalizations (and laws) to observations; that is, they are statements of regularities in those observations.[2] The relation between such statements and theories is not so simple, however. Regarding this relation, there appear to be at least two distinct views. One of these argues that theories are generated, not inductively from empirical generalizations, but by the invention and manipulation of experientially meaningless symbols. For example, Watson claims that although the paths by which theories are reached "are very diverse and dependent upon a variety of coincidences," the principal path runs as follows:

> At first we operate only with thought abstractions, mindful of our task only to construct inner representation-pictures. Proceeding in this way, we do not as yet take possible experiential facts into consideration, but merely make the effort to develop our thought-pictures with as much clarity as possible and to draw from them all possible consequences. Only subsequently, after the entire exposition of the picture has been completed, do we check its agreement with experiential facts (1960:249).

Popper also denies the systematic bearing of empirical generalizations on theorizing by taking a position that "stands directly opposed to all attempts to operate with the ideas of inductive logic" (1961:30). In fact, he argues that there is *no* logic for generating theories:

> My view of the matter, for what it is worth, is that there is no such thing as a logical method of having new ideas, or a logical reconstruction of this process. My view may be expressed by saying that every discovery contains "an irrational element," or "a creative intuition," in Bergson's sense. In a similar way Einstein speaks of the "search for those highly universal laws . . . from which a picture of the world can be obtained by pure deduction. There is no logical path," he says, "leading to these . . . laws. They can only be reached

2. See Kaplan (1964:85-94) for some roles of empirical generalizations other than those discussed here; and the same author (1964:94-115) for various kinds of empirical generalizations. See Wartofsky (1968:252-258) for an exposition of realist, nominalist, and conceptualist views of "the nature of the laws of nature."

by intuition, based upon something like an intellectual love ("*Einfühlung*") of the objects of experience" (1961:32).

In Popper's view, however, the absence of a logic for *generating* theories does not matter. What matters is the logic for *testing* theories, necessitated by the centrality of criticism in the scientific process and by the injunction "that whenever we try to propose a solution to a problem, we ought to try as hard as we can to overthrow our solution rather than defend it" (1961:16).

Clearly, then, Popper's main argument vigorously denies the role of inductive logic in how particular theories are verified,[3] and denies the role of any logic — whether inductive or not — in how particular theories are generated. Nevertheless, Popper does admit of a "quasi-inductive" process in the historical evolution of science as a whole. In this process, he says:

> Theories of some level of generality are proposed, and deductively tested; after that, theories of a higher level of universality are proposed, and in their turn tested with the help of those of the previous levels of universality, and so on. The methods of testing are invariably based on deductive inferences from the higher to the lower level; on the other hand, the levels of universality are reached, in the order of time, by proceeding from lower to higher levels (1961:276-277).

In marked contrast to Watson's and Popper's characterization of theorizing as a process that responds to empirical generalizations only after it has been fully developed in its logical aspects, Merton argues:

> It is my central thesis that empirical research goes far beyond the passive role of verifying and testing theory; it does more than confirm or refute hypotheses. Research plays an active role: it performs at least four major functions which help shape the devel-

3. "I never assume that we can argue from the truth of singular statements to the truth of theories. I never assume that by force of "verified" conclusions, theories can be established as "true", or even as merely probable" (Popper, 1961:33).

opment of theory. It *initiates,* it *reformulates,* it *deflects,* and it *clarifies* theory (1957:103).

Kuhn's position is similar to Merton's inasmuch as he locates the stimulus for theorizing almost entirely in the "anomaly" and "crisis" that is occasioned by an unanticipated empirical generalization.[4] But as Popper's reference to quasi-induction in science (mentioned above) implicitly moderates his view in the direction of Kuhn, so Kuhn's acknowledgement that "how an individual invents (or finds that he has invented) a new way of giving order to data now all assembled — must here remain inscrutable and may be permanently so" (1964:89), moderates toward Popper. Kuhn says:

> Discovery commences with the awareness of anomaly, i.e., with the recognition that nature has somehow violated the paradigm-induced expectations that govern normal science. It then continues with a more or less extended exploration of the area of anomaly. And it closes only when the paradigm theory has been adjusted so that the anomalous has become the expected. Assimilating a new sort of fact demands a more than additive adjustment of theory, and until that adjustment is completed — until the scientist has learned to see nature in a different way — the new fact is not quite a scientific fact at all (1964:52-53).

Nagel, however, believes that the contrast is more apparent than real:

> Distinguished scientists have repeatedly claimed that theories are "free creations of the mind." Such claims obviously do not mean

4. For another discussion of anomalous, unpredicted, empirical generalizations, see Merton (1957:103-108). In fact, Merton (although closely identified with functional structuralism, a theoretic viewpoint wherein the accurate anticipation of actions and reactions is an essential explanation of social phenomena) pays special attention to unanticipated phenomena of various kinds throughout his work. His well-known discussion of serendipity in research is but one example; another is his distinction between manifest and latent functions; a third, although more implicit, example is his typology of deviant behaviors.

that theories may not be *suggested* by observational materials or that theories do not require support from observational evidence. What such claims do rightly assert is that the basic terms of a theory need not possess meanings which are fixed by definite experimental procedures, and that a theory may be adequate and fruitful despite the fact that the evidence for it is necessarily indirect (1961:86).

Concept Formation and Proposition Formation

In short, therefore, theories may be viewed as emerging by making the terms and relationships in empirical generalizations more abstract, and also by introducing other abstract terms that refer to nonobservable constructs. Both procedures are referred to as concept formation. As noted in Chapter 1, the empirical generalization that a higher suicide rate is associated with Protestant than with Catholic church affiliation can become more fully theoretic in the statement that the incidence of deviant behavior is caused by the degree of egoism. In this case, "suicide rate" is made more abstract in the term "incidence of deviant behavior"; "Protestant-versus-Catholic church affiliation" is made more abstract in the term "egoism"; and "is associated with" is replaced by the construct, "is caused by."

As this illustration shows, theoretic concepts are formed by naming various sorts of things. Hempel (1952, 1965) has discussed three different procedures for doing so that may be summarized as follows: First, conceptual naming can be of *all* of the observables, but only the observables, to be included under each individual name or term. This concept formation procedure is typical of operationalism as advocated by Bridgman. It involves a closed relation of concept to observables such that each concept refers only to a limited, specified, set of observables (and, in the operationalist view, a limited, specified set of the unique operations necessary to produce these observations). If either the concept or its corresponding set of observables is changed, then the other must be changed. Thus, for extreme example, if "intelligence" is defined as an individual's achievement of a given score on a particular test, his scores on any other similar, but not identical, tests would require naming new concepts for each.

Second, conceptual naming can be of *some* of the observables, but only observables, to be included under each individual name or term. This procedure involves the use of "reduction sentences" and involves a more open relation of concept to observables insofar as the concept is reduced to an indeterminate, and only partially specified, set of observables. In other words, concept formation by reduction sentences allows for provisionally specifying the observational referents of a concept, without closing the concept to other referents that may be added to it in the future. Hempel points out that "sets of reduction sentences combine in a peculiar way the functions of concept formation and theory formation" (1952:28), since the criterion for adding new observational referents to a given concept seems to be the empirical correlation of these new referents with the referent named in the first reduction sentence. In Hempel's words,

> While a single reduction sentence may be viewed simply as laying down a notational convention for the use of the term (i.e., the concept) it introduces, this is no longer possible for a set of two or more reduction sentences concerning the same term, because such a set implies, as a rule, certain statements which have the character of empirical laws; such a set cannot be used in science unless there is evidence to support the laws in question (1952:28).

Thus, one could legitimately add scores on different tests as observational referents of "intelligence" only on evidence (perhaps such as factor analysis would provide) that they were highly correlated with score on the original test. As more and more such intercorrelated referents were added, the concept "intelligence" would come increasingly to resemble a theory — that is, a set of interrelated empirical propositions. Finally,

according to Hempel, conceptual naming can be of both observables and *non*observables (for example, dispositions such as
"magnetism" or "charisma," or metrical terms such as "temperature, pressure, volume" or "class, status, power"), not one
at a time as in the previous two concept formation procedures,
but in theoretically related *sets*.[5]

> Terms of this [latter] kind are not introduced by definitions or
> reduction chains based on observables; in fact, they are not intro-
> duced by any piecemeal process of assigning meaning to them
> individually. Rather, the constructs used in a theory are introduced
> jointly, as it were, by setting up a theoretical system formulated in
> terms of them and by giving this system an experiential interpreta-
> tion which in turn confers empirical meaning on the theoretical
> constructs (1952:32).

Once the required and appropriate observables and unob-
servables have been conceptualized, propositions are formed by
fitting them into the form, "If concept X, then concept Y," or
"The greater the X, the greater the Y." Two contrasting features of such a theoretic proposition emerge as a result of its
high degree of abstraction: the scope of the relationship claimed
in the empirical generalization from which the proposition was
generated is increased; but at the same time, its empirical ambiguity is also increased. In other words, the originally observed
relationship is made tentatively applicable to more phenomena
than are referred to in the generalization from which the theoretic proposition is induced, thus presenting an opportunity to
broaden the scope of the information contained therein.[6] For

5. Wilson and Dumont refer to this procedure as utilizing "translation
rules" (1968). See also Dumont and Wilson (1967).
6. Merton cites five "functions of theory" vis-a-vis empirical research.
The first is that "the *scope* of the original empirical finding is considerably
extended (by theory), and several seemingly disparate uniformities are seen
to be interrelated. . . ." The second also specifies a consequence of transforming empirical generalizations into theory: "Once having established the theoretic pertinence of a uniformity by deriving it from a set of interrelated

the same reasons, however, the precise additional observations and empirical generalizations (and therefore the precise methods) to which the theoretic proposition is actually applicable are far less clear than is the case with the originating empirical generalization. Because of this, the choice of new empirical observations ("indicators") to which the theoretic proposition is presumed to be applicable is a crucial step in testing the truth and scope of the theory.

In addition to heightened abstraction, the transformation from empirical generalization to theory involves heightened idealization insofar as error terms that are usually explicit in the former are dropped or relegated to an implicit status in the latter. Such terms may represent both measurement error and the impingement of exogenous factors on the variables being studied,[7] and without them, theoretic propositions take on a typically universal and unequivocal character. This idealization seems to have two opposing consequences:

On the one hand, theories acquire a stubborn resistance to change. Because error terms are routinely dropped before empirical findings are incorporated into theoretic propositions, the theory may not immediately reflect any increase in the error of its predictions — especially so long as these predictions continue to be borne out in general direction.

---

propositions, we provide for the *cumulation* both of theory and of research findings. . . ." The third, fourth, and fifth, however, seem more properly to specify consequences of the next transformation shown in Figure 1 above: namely, that of theory into hypotheses: "3. The conversion of empirical uniformities into theoretic statements . . . increases the *fruitfulness* of research through the successive exploration of implications. 4. By providing a rationale, the theory introduces a *ground for prediction* which is more secure than mere empirical extrapolation from previously observed trends. 5. If theory is to be productive, it must be sufficiently *precise* to be *determinate* (and) precision enhances the likelihood of approximating a 'crucial' observation or experiment" (1957:97-99).

7. For discussions of "exogenous variables" or "contingencies lying outside a given context," see Blalock (1968:48ff) and Bohm (1961:20-25, 141-143, 158).

But on the other hand, no matter how stubbornly theories resist change, they also and simultaneously encourage their own exposure to change-inducing external factors. Because universality and unequivocality is claimed for theories, they are presumed applicable to new contexts and with new techniques. It is precisely here, in such new applications, that new exogenous variables and new measurement errors are encountered, with resulting new opportunities for empirical discoveries and technical inventions that can bring about change in theory.

Proposition Arrangement and Theories

When propositions having these qualities of abstraction and idealization are arranged into a logical deductive system or a causal concatenation (discussed in Chapter 6,)the resulting structure is termed a "theory." From this structure two consequences flow: (1) theories can *explain* known empirical generalizations; and (2) theories can *predict* empirical generalizations that are still unknown. In other words, when the set of propositions that are yielded by conceptual transformation of known empirical generalizations are arranged in a specifiable form — especially a deductive form — then not only can the original empirical generalizations be explained but also new and untested empirical generalizations can be predicted or hypothesized.[8]

Such are the basic functions of theory within the scientific process in general. Because of these functions, theories are also

8. Braithwaite defines "the hypothetico-deductive method" as that of deducing the hypothesis in question from higher-level hypotheses which have themselves been inductively established (1960:261). And Nagel says, "Explanation of already established experimental laws is [one] function theories are expected to perform. Another role played by theories which differentiates them from experimental laws is to provide suggestions for fresh experimental laws" (1961:89-90). See also Greer (1969:123) and Dubin (1969:10-25, ,03), although Dubin prefers "understanding" to "explanation." On the latter two terms, see Kaplan (1964:335).

directly relevant to particular empirical researches at two points in their developmental histories: theories specify the factors one should be able to measure *before* doing empirical research; and *after* the research is done, theories serve as common languages into which the findings (that is, the empirical generalizations) of many researches may be translated for purposes of test, comparison, and logical integration. These appear to be the two closely related functions of theory that Merton and Homans, respectively, have in mind. Merton stresses the *pre* research function: "Concepts [the elements that are interrelated in a theory] constitute the definitions (or prescriptions) of what is to be observed; they are the variables between which empirical relationships are to be sought" (1957:89). Homans stresses the *post* research function by quoting Willard Gibbs' statement: "It is the office of theoretical investigation to give the form in which the results of experiment may be expressed" (1950:441). Zetterberg also takes note of these two functions of theory: "A theory can be used to locate the most strategic or manageable propositions for testing" (1963:77), and "A theory can be used to provide the most parsimonious summary of actual or anticipated research findings" (1963:75).[9] Theories thus face the past as well as the future of a science by summarizing the information the science has already systematized and by guiding its efforts to systematize still more. Hempel offers this summary image:

> A scientific theory might therefore be likened to a complex spatial network: Its terms are represented by the knots, while the threads connecting the latter correspond, in part, to the definitions and, in part, to the fundamental derivative hypotheses included in the theory. The whole system floats, as it were, above the plane of observation and is anchored to it by rules of interpretation. These

9. (See also Kaplan (1964:302.) These are Zetterberg's first and third "virtues" of theorizing. His second ("A theory can be used to coordinate research. . . .") and fourth ("A theory provides a limited area in which to test false propositions. . . .") seem to be elaborations on the first.

might be viewed as strings which are not part of the network but link certain points of the latter with specific places in the plane of observation. By virtue of those interpretive connections, the network can function as a scientific theory: From certain observational data, we may ascend, via an interpretive string, to some point in the theoretical network, thence proceed, via definitions and hypotheses, to other points, from which another interpretive string permits a descent to the plane of observation (1952:36).

Chapter Four

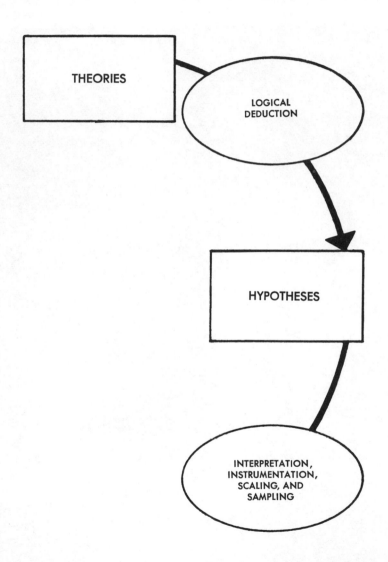

Theories; Logical Deduction; Hypotheses; Interpretation, Instrumentation, Scaling, and Sampling

Theories

Figure 2 indicates that at this point in the scientific process the construction of theory from observations ends and the application of theory to observations begins. Theories are not all equally applicable to given observations, however, and the extent to which a given theory provides useful symbolic representation of observations both actual and possible (and is, in this sense, applicable to them) seems to depend on at least three kinds of test comparisons. First, internal comparisons may be made, whereby some parts of the theory are compared with other parts in order to test whether the theory is internally consistent and nontautological. Second, the theory may be compared with other theories in order to test whether, all other things being equal, it would be informationally superior to them by having broader conceptual scope, or higher conceptual abstraction, by being more parsimonious, or by having greater language determinacy, universality, flexibility or abstractness (see Chapter 6). Third, the theory may be compared with empirical facts by comparing its predictions or low-level hypotheses with appropriate empirical generalizations in order to test the truth of the theory.

The placement of "hypotheses" in Figure 1 (that is, as deductive products of theories which are themselves partly the products of induction) is meant to reflect such opinions as Feigl's, who defines "prediction" as a "form of deductive inference from inductive premises" (1953:418). Note that I use "prediction" synonymously with "hypothesis" in this discussion. It should be understood, however, that what is intended is an explicitly deductive prediction, rather than simply an extrapolative or interpolative prediction from known empirical generalizations and laws.[1] Given this intended meaning, "hypothesis" is in better accord with current usage in sociology, where "prediction" almost always refers to observable *events* that have not yet occurred, while "hypothesis" refers to *observations* that have not yet been made — whether on past, present, or future events. It is the latter reference that is intended here by both terms.[2]

Logical Deduction and Hypotheses

Evaluating the formal utility of a theory is a relatively easy task; essentially, one works with a library, paper, pencil, and the rules of logic. But the substantive truth of a theory is much more difficult to assess because of the multiplicity and complexity of the procedures that are required. As Figure 1 indicates, the first step is to deduce hypotheses from the theory. The

1. For a brief discussion of predictive studies in sociology, see Lazarsfeld and Rosenberg 1955:204-205; and for discussion of predicting observations from empirical generalizations, see Nagel 1961:63 and Dubin 1969:14-18.
2. Regarding the former reference, of "prediction" to future events, Feigl adds that "The one remarkable feature in which social-science predictions differ from those in the natural sciences is the well-known fact that once these predictions have been divulged, their very existence (that is, their being taken cognizance of) may upset the original prediction" (1953:418). For the classic discussion of this feature, see Merton on "The Self-Fulfilling Prophecy" (1957:421-436). In an extension of this idea to life in general, Bohm says, "A fundamental property of life is that the very processes that are necessary for its existence will change it" (1961:152).

crucial importance of low-level hypotheses to testing the truth of theories is expressed by Braithwaite:

> Taking all the highest-level hypotheses of a scientific system together, the grounds for believing them are no more and no less than the fact that the lowest-level hypotheses deduced from them are confirmed by experience (1960:352).

In Popper's terms:

> Certain singular statements — which we may call "predictions" — are deduced from the theory, especially predictions that are easily testable or applicable . . . . Next we seek a decision as regards these (and other) derived statements by comparing them with the results of practical applications and experiments. If this decision is positive, that is, if the singular conclusions turn out to be acceptable, or *verified,* then the theory has for the time being, passed its test: we have found no reason to discard it. But if the decision is negative, or in other words, if the conclusions have been falsified, then their falsification also falsifies the theory from which they were logically deduced (1961:33).

Thus, from a theory claiming that:

(1) An increase in the number of associates per member will produce an increase in the division of labor;
(2) An increase in the division of labor will produce an increase in solidarity;
(3) An increase in solidarity will produce an increase in consensus;
(4) An increase in solidarity will produce a decrease in the number of rejections of deviants (Blalock, 1969:19).

one could deduce that:

(5) An increase in the number of associates per member will produce a decrease in the number of rejections of deviants; and
(6) An increase in consensus will be associated with a decrease in number of rejections of deviants.[3]

3. These deductions assume that the minimum requirements suggested by Costner and Leik have been met, specifically including the assumption of

Assuming that a given theory is internally no less consistent and nontautological than other comparable theories, and that it is not informationally inferior to them, the extent to which its deduced hypotheses accord with pertinent empirical generalizations will determine, ideally, its scientific acceptance.

Interpretation

However, as Nagel points out, theoretically deduced predictions or hypotheses do not lead immediately and unambiguously to observations:

> If [a] theory is to be used as an instrument of explanation and prediction, it must somehow be linked with observable materials.
>
> The indispensability of such linkages has been repeatedly stressed in recent literature, and a variety of labels have been coined for them: coordinating definitions, operational definitions, semantical rules, correspondence rules, epistemic correlations, and rules of interpretation (1961:93).

In short, observable indicators must be identified for at least some of the abstract concepts contained in a theory before the hypothetical predictions of a theory (and, by inference, the theory itself) can be tested.[4] Zetterberg offers an illustration from sociology:

> Suppose that we are interested in the verification of the hypothesis: *The greater the division of labor is in a society, the less the rejection of deviates in the same society.* For its verification we first need to interpret the nominal definitions of an hypothesis into terms more acceptable for research. We may, for example, select the number of occupations to stand for the division of labor. And we may select the proportion of laws requiring the death penalty, deportation and

---

"a 'closed system,' i.e., there is no 'connection' (causal or 'spurious') between the variables in the postulates except those stated or implied in the postulates" (1964:831). Further, it is assumed that none of the variables have "critical" or "threshold" values that limit their effects on other variables.

4. Hempel says "An adequate empirical interpretation turns a theoretical system into a testable theory: The hypotheses whose constituent terms have been interpreted become capable of test by reference to observable phenomena" (1952:35).

long prison terms (but not fines) to stand for the degree of rejection of deviates from society norms. These interpretations of the nominal definitions we term *operational definitions*. Operational we call the definitions that refer to measurements or enumerations (1954: 29 – 30).[5]

In general, the process of interpreting a theoretic hypothesis (and thereby restating that hypothesis in empirically testable form) follows the reverse of the "concept formation" procedures discussed above. Thus, instead of naming observables and theoretic constructs, as in concept formation, one interprets hypotheses by specifying observables and metrics to which the concepts contained in these hypotheses are taken to refer.

In discussing the problem of interpretation, Blalock stresses that the distance between "main or general" theories (cast in the "theoretical language in which we do our thinking") and "auxiliary" theories (cast in "operational language involving explicit instructions for classifying or measuring") cannot be closed by logic alone. "instead, a correspondence between two concepts, one in each language, must be established by common agreement or *a priori* assumption" (1968:23-24; see also Blalock 1969: 151-154). Because of this unavoidably conventional, rather than logical or empirical, quality that inheres in the process whereby theoretic propostions are interpreted, Blalock argues that "no deductively formulated theory or any proposi-

5. Zetterberg also notes that one result of interpreting a theoretic hypothesis is a "working hypothesis. This is the hypothesis we subject to empirical test" (1954:31). It is at this point that the questions of validity and reliability come to the fore: "If the operational definitions have perfect reliability and validity, then, and only then, the working hypothesis is identical with the original hypothesis" (1954:31). See also his fuller discussion of these questions (1964:42-52). Dubin refers to an interpreted theoretic proposition as simply "an hypothesis" (1969:212-215). See also Dubin's discussions of operationism and reliability, and of validity (185-188 and 206-210). Kaplan (1964:88) distinguishes between a "working hypothesis" ("A belief pertaining to the course of inquiry but not necessarily pertaining to its ultimate destination") and a "test hypothesis" ("This is what we think may very well be the truth of the matter, and we then organize the inquiry so as to facilitate the decision on whether the conjecture is correct.") I follow Kaplan's usage here.

tions in that theory are ever directly testable" (1968:11). It is thus only by common consent among scientists (with all the familiar sociological influences to which that consent must be subject) that any given "auxiliary" theory comes to be accepted as a legitimate interpretation of any given "main" theory.

But once an interpretation is put forward in a given research, the resultant "test" hypothesis (or "auxiliary theory") must be instrumented, and a measurement scale and sampling procedure must be applied to it. To use Zetterberg's illustration regarding the division of labor and the rejection of deviates, this means that the researcher may decide to make observations on "the number of occupations" and, say, "the proportion of laws requiring the death penalty, deportation, and long prison terms" by interviewing or by mailing questionnaires to or reading the publications of persons designated as competent judges (for example, census officials and officials in the legal system); or by directly observing social actors as they fill their occupational and legal roles in the field; or by setting up an experimental situation in which he rigorously controls the occupations and laws to which his subjects can respond; or by devising a simulation in which occupations and laws are represented by electrical inputs into a computer;[6] or in any number of other ways. Each way will involve its own distinctive set of observational instruments, scales, and sampling techniques. Let us briefly consider each of these.

Instrumentation

The instruments whereby observations are made are divisible into two general classes involving (1) human sensory organs unaugmented by technologies other than skill; and (2) technologically augmented sensory organs. To illustrate: the tech-

6. See Zetterberg (1963:78-82) for a discussion of "allegories" and other simulations.

nique called "participant observation" relies primarily on the first class of instruments (that is, unaided but well-trained eyes, ears, nose, etc., although they may be minimally augmented by collecting artifacts, taking notes, photographs, tape recordings, and the like). On the other hand, in the technique called "social survey," technological augmentation of direct sensory perception is central insofar as primary observational reliance falls on the paper-and-pencil questionnaire or interview schedule.

Technological augmentation of the senses seems to be a general trend in all sciences as we seek, more and more, to make observations on phenomena that are not immediately available to an observer's senses (for example, gravitational and electromagnetic fields, values, attitudes) and to raise the precision of all our observations. The price that is paid for this additional scope and precision is chiefly in the additional observational error introduced by the unavoidable indirectness of technologically augmented observation. For example, light passes through manufactured lenses (and often onto a photographic plate, etc.) before reaching the astronomer's eye; and a respondent's age or occupation or attitude passes through his own and the interviewer's sometimes-censoring (or simply mistaken) consciousness and often hard-to-read writing or hard-to-understand tape recording before reaching the survey analyst's eye or ear. Thus, although one can see "farther" with a telescope than with the naked eye, and one can collect more information more quickly from a questionnaire than from direct observation of a respondent, the images projected by telescope and questionnaire may be more distorted (and are certainly differently distorted) than those built up by unaugmented observation.

Scaling

Whether the observational instruments are technologically augmented or not, they all seem to comprise both a mechanism for receiving signals (such as, light, sound, verbal and nonverbal gestures) and a scale against which the signals or their symbolic representations (for example, a pointer on a dial, an "X" in a box) may be compared for purposes of measurement. As indicated earlier, a "scale" is a set of abstract symbols that can be systematically attached to concrete observations thereby "measuring" the observations. The range of symbols that can constitute a scale is limitless: the names of two or more colors is a scale, the signs of the zodiac is a scale, "yes-no" is a scale. As Nagel points out: "A numerical evaluation of things is only one way of making evaluations of certain selected characters, although it is so far the best" [7] (1960:122). " '*This* is the missing book,' or 'He had a *good* sleep,' or 'The cake is *too* sweet,' are judgments making no explicit reference to number. From this larger point of view, measurement can be regarded as the delimitation and fixation of our ideas of things, so that the determination of what it is to be a man or to be a circle is a case of measurement" (1960:121).

More generally, Wartofsky points out that:

> Once concept formation and language attain to the ideas of *thing* and *same* and *different*, discourse already exhibits the notion of *class* as an ordering concept . . . . Here measurement already has its roots, in the process of identification, comparison, and classification . . . . The refinement of these basic measurement concepts is one of the greatest of human achievements, often providing the

7. Kaplan's view is somewhat narrower: "Measurement, in most general terms, can be regarded as the assignment of numbers to objects (or events or situations) in accord with some rule" (1964:177). But he also speaks of measurement as "the mapping of objects into an abstract space" and notes that "the space into which objects are mapped need not consist of numbers. Generally speaking, it would be more accurate to say that what is assigned to each object is a *numeral* rather than a number. The rule of assignment determines certain relationships among the numerals, and it is this pattern of relationships which constitutes the abstract space" (1964:177-178).

instrumentalities for technological change and social transformation (1968:153,154).

Four general types of scales have been described by Stevens (1946), whose discussion may be summarized as follows.[8] Stevens bases his description on the claim that "Scales are possible in the first place and because there is a certain isomorphism between what we can do with the aspects of objects and the properties of the numeral series" (1946:142). It follows that "what we can do with the aspects of objects" limits the type of scale that can be employed. Thus, if we can determine only whether the relevant aspects of objects are the same or different (equality-inequality), then the only legitimate type of scale is "nominal." The legitimate manipulations (in Stevens' terms, the "permissible statistics") with such a scale are, in turn, limited to computing the number of cases, the mode, and contingency correlations. In sociological research, nominal scales are represented, for example, by codes for the race, sex, and political preference of respondent, and for such aspects of groups as are referred to in Bales' interaction process categories (1950)

Now, if in addition to equality-inequality, we can make determinations of greater-or-less-than between aspects of objects, then the appropriate type of scale is "ordinal." Here the permissible statistics include all those for nominal scales plus the median and percentiles. Ordinal scales are represented, for example, by some scales for social class (when the determinable difference between classes are of the "upper," "middle," "lower" type) and attitudes (when the determinable differences are of the "approve-disapprove" type).

Further, if in addition to greater-or-less-than, we can determine equality-inequality in the differences or intervals between the aspects of objects, then the appropriate type of scale is "interval." The permissible statistics for such a scale include all

8. See also Kaplan (1964:191-198), and Wartofsky (1968:153-172).

those previously mentioned, plus the mean standard deviation, rank-order correlation, and product-moment correlation. Interval scales are represented, for example, by some scales for social class (when the determinable differences between such aspects are of the type described in Duncan [1961]), attitudes (under such manipulations as are indicated in Guttman scaling [1950]), and many collective measures, such as average group income.

Finally, if in addition to all of the preceding determinations, we can also determine equality-inequality in the ratios of aspects of objects, then the appropriate type of scale is "ratio." Of ratio scales, Stevens says:

> Once such a scale is erected, its numerical values can be transformed (as from inches to feet) only by multiplying each value by a constant. An absolute zero is always implied, even though the zero value on some scales (e.g., Absolute Temperature) may never be produced. All types of statistical measures are applicable to ratio scales, and only with these scales may we properly indulge in logarithmic transformations such as are involved in the use of decibels.
>
> Foremost among the ratio scales is the scale of number itself — cardinal number — the scale we use when we count such things as eggs, pennies, and apples. This scale of the numerosity of aggregates is so basic and so common that it is ordinarily not even mentioned in discussions of measurement (1946:147).

Thus, ratio scales are employed in measuring such sociologically relevant aspects as size of population, number of births, number of deaths, annual income, age, and the like.

Within the range provided by these four general types of scales, there exists a host of systematic, conventionalized, and near-universal techniques for transforming observations into empirical generalizations. One can select a scale that already exists or construct a new one, and a major part of a scientist's training stresses the procedures for doing both.[9]

9. Note that the scale one uses to measure a given observation seems to

Sampling

Finally, in addition to specifying observable indicators of abstract concepts *(interpretation),* devising or selecting appropriate *instruments* with which these indicators are to be observed, and devising or selecting a *scale* for measuring the observations, the investigator must make certain decisions regarding the *sample* of observables on which observations are to be made.[10] That is, the researcher must define the population to which he wishes to apply his anticipated empirical generalizations (for example, in studying the division of labor in society, should the "society" in question be U.S. or Haitian society? In the eighteenth century or the twentieth century?). He must then decide whether to make observations on a representative or a purposive sample of observable occupations and laws in that society; and he must decide how to draw this sample.

From what has just been said, it should be clear that the methodological controls of interpretation, instrumentation, scaling, and sampling are oriented not only to the making of observations, but also to the next methodological steps (measurement, sample summarization, and parameter estimation) and the next information component (empirical generalizations) in the scientific process. Thus, the trained investigator anticipates and prepares for his measurement procedures through his interpretation, instrumentation, and scaling procedures; and in the same way, he anticipates and prepares for his

----

depend on the design of one's research (that is, on the hypothesis being tested, available instrumentation and hypothesis-testing techniques, etc.) rather than on any intrinsic characteristics of the observable itself. For example, the colors of visible light may be measured by their names (nominal scale) or by their wave lengths (ratio scale); occupational prestige may be measured by a "high-medium-low" ordinal scale or by the Hatt-North (1947) interval scale, etc. See the suggestion to this general effect, even at the level of wave-particle duality in physics, in Bohm (1961:138). For an apparently opposing view, see Dubin (1969:35).

10. See Lazerwitz (1968) for a discussion of the logic and procedures of sampling.

sample summarization and parameter estimation procedures through his sampling procedures. Such anticipation and preparation is largely what is meant by good research design.

Chapter Five

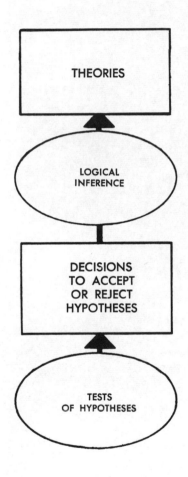

THEORIES

LOGICAL
INFERENCE

DECISIONS
TO ACCEPT
OR REJECT
HYPOTHESES

TESTS
OF HYPOTHESES

Tests of Hypotheses;
Decisions to Accept or Reject
Hypotheses; Logical Inference;
Theories

Tests of Hypotheses

At this point, in terms of Figure 1, we have come again to "observations"; and the comments made above, on observations, empirical generalizations, and their respective methodological controls, apply once again. Consequently, let us assume that new findings (that is, new empirical generalizations), whose form has been constructed to correspond logically to a given theoretically-deduced hypothesis, have been generated. Two further steps are now taken: (1) the finding is compared with the hypothesis[1] and a decision is made on whether the "fit" of the latter to the former is satisfactory; and (2) that fit or lack of fit is inferred (induced) as confirmation or falsification (including modification) of the theory from which the hypothesis was deduced. Thus, Popper argues: "What ultimately decides the fate of a theory is the result of a test" (1961:109). "The

---

1. Zetterberg defines "the verification enterprise" as "a comparison of two broad classes of sentences, those in a theory and those about indicators and data" (1963:36). See Zetterberg (1963:37-42, 56-82) for an account of the test procedure. See Popper (1961:68-92) for a discussion of falsification as the basic test procedure. See Kaplan (1964:37) for a brief comparison of verification and falsification, and for a summary of Reichenbach's three kinds of tests: technical, physical, and logical.

testing of a theory depends upon basic statements whose acceptance or rejection, in its turn, depends upon our decisions. Thus it is *decisions* which settle the fate of theories" (1961:108).

It is important to point out, however, that hypotheses vary widely in the extent to which they *can* be tested, both in principle and in practice. A hypothesis is testable in principle if it predicts that at least one logically possible empirical generalization will not be found to be true in fact; and the more such predictions it makes or implies, the more readily testable it is. In other words, a hypothesis is highly testable in principle when it can be shown to be false by any of a large number of logically possible empirical findings and when only one or a few such findings can confirm it. For a simple example, the hypothesis that "all human groups are either stratified or not stratified" is untestable in principle because it does not rule out any logically possible empirical findings. The hypothesis that "all human groups are stratified," however, is testable because it asserts that the discovery of an unstratified human group, though logically possible, will not in fact occur. Further, the hypothesis that "all human groups are stratified according to prestige rank" is still more testable, since it rules out and can be falsified by even more logically possible findings — that some human groups are not stratified at all, or that some are stratified but not according to prestige rank.

Popper graphically describes the falsifiability (in-principle testability) of hypotheses, and argues that its maximization is essential to the overall progress of a science:

> If . . . we represent the class of all possible basic statements by a circular area, and the possible event by the radii of the circle, then we can say: At least *one* radius — or perhaps better, one narrow sector . . . — must be incompatible with the theory and ruled out by it. One might then represent the potential falsifiers of various theories by sectors of various widths. . . .
>
> Let us now imagine that we are given a theory, and that . . . the

basic statements *not* forbidden by the theory will be represented by a narrow remaining sector. . . . A theory like this would obviously be very easy to falsify, since it allows the empirical world only a narrow range of possibilities; for it rules out almost all conceivable, i.e. logically possible, events. It asserts so much about the world of experience, "its empirical content is so great," that there is, as it were, little chance for it to escape falsification.

Now theoretical science aims, precisely, at obtaining theories which are easily falsifiable in this sense . . . . If we could be successful in obtaining a theory such as this, then this theory would describe "our particular world" as precisely as a theory can; for it would single out the world of "our experience" from the class of all logically possible worlds of experience with the greatest precision attainable by theoretical science (1961:112-113).

Assuming that a hypothesis is testable in principle, it is testable in practice if the requisite observations, empirical generalizations, and tests can actually be made, given the nature of the phenomena to be investigated, and given a particular available scientific technology (or, more generally, methods, including interpretation, instrumentation, sampling, scaling, and measurement techniques).

Blalock has dealt specifically with some testability problems encountered in sociology, where it is extremely difficult to isolate any given system of variables from disturbances originating outside that system and where hypotheses are therefore often phrased in very imprecise "tendency" terms. Accordingly, Blalock points out that:

When we state laws in statistical terms, allowing for large amounts of unexplained variation, it becomes much more difficult to develop deductive systems. For example, the simple line of reasoning, if A then B, if B then C, therefore if A then C becomes translated into if A then usually B, if B then usually C, therefore if A then sometimes C. Such a theory no longer has much predictive value, unless precise values can be supplied for the probability of B given A, and so forth (1968:156).

Blalock argues that an alternative to imprecise statistical laws, however, is to formulate

> . . . deductive theories that apply only to ideal models. But how would these theories be tested? . . . The testing of exactly formulated deductive theories depends . . . on our being able to approximate the ideal conditions specified. Laboratory experiments are not necessary if one can find natural systems that are for all practical purposes effectively isolated from outside influences. . . . Let us assume that in the foreseeable future sociologists will seldom find it possible to test theories under any such ideal conditions. It remains possible that the best strategy is to formulate rather precise deductive theories but to be satisfied with very crude tests of such theories. Another alternative — which may turn out in many instances to be equivalent to the first — is to construct deductive theories that allow for unexplained variation. . . . But as soon as we begin to allow for such disturbances, we must make certain simplifying assumptions about *how* they are related to the other variables. Otherwise . . . testable predictions cannot be made (1968:157).

And regarding such simplifying assumptions, Blalock notes that:

> . . . the scientist is always confronted with the dilemma of how much to oversimplify reality. On the one hand, simple theories are easier to construct and evaluate. On the other hand, the more complex ones may stand a better chance of conforming to reality (1968:159).

Assuming that this dilemma is at least provisionally resolved with respect to a given hypothesis and assuming that one is satisfied with the testability of that hypothesis, both in principle and in practice, then its actual test can proceed.

Decisions to Accept or Reject Hypotheses

Popper suggests (1961:109-110) that the test procedure is analogous to trial by jury, wherein the truth of an allegation of hypothesis is decided according to certain rules of evidence and procedure, and to sentence by a judge, wherein the fate of the actor of whom the allegation is made, or of the theory from which the hypothesis is deduced, is determined.

In the "trial" phase, the scientist takes into systematic account (1) the originating theory, its prior support, and the steps by which the hypothesis in question was deduced (usually summarized in the "statement of the problem" and "review of the literature" sections of his research report); and (2) the interpretation, scaling, instrumentation, and sampling steps that were involved in producing individual observations, and the measurements, sample summarization, and parameter estimation steps that were involved in producing the relevant empirical generalizations (usually summarized in the "methods" section). By systematic criticism of these information components and methodological controls, prior to performing the actual comparison of empirical finding to theoretic hypothesis, the scientist seeks to evaluate the extent to which the two *can* be compared. That is, at this point the scientist wishes to know: How well integrated and well established is the theory? How carefully deduced is the hypothesis? How inventively, rigorously, and communicably has it been interpreted, scaled, instrumented, and directed to a known sample of a specifiable population? How much in accord with established (or establishable) procedures of measurement, sample summarization, and parameter estimation has been the induction of observations to empirical generalizations? In short, do the findings provide a fair test of the hypotheses? If the balance of each answer is positive, then the next step is the test or comparison itself. Here, a central problem is to establish an "objective" (that is, intersubjectively agreed–upon–in–advance) measure of whatever fit may exist between fact and hypotheses, and an "objective" set of rules for taking that measurement.

Statistical tests provide the most "objective," most rigorous, and most sensitive rules available for measuring the fit between hypothesis and finding. For such tests, both the hypothesis and the finding must be expressed in quantitative form, and this is unfortunately not always the case. Without such statistical tests, however, we are forced back upon authoritarian, or mystical, or logico-rational, or perhaps aesthetic, appeals.

Logical Inference and Theories

Regardless of how the decision is made regarding the fit of hypothesis to finding, however, the next step is judgmental, inferentially bringing this decision to bear upon the theory from which the hypothesis was deduced.[2] In general, the decision is judged to (1) "lend confirmation to" the theory by not disconfirming it; (2) "modify" the theory by disconfirming it, but not at a crucial point;[3] or (3) "overthrow" the theory by disconfirming it at a crucial point in its logical structure, in its history of competition with rival theories.[4] The alternative that is inferred, and its degree,[5] depends upon the test decision itself and the importance that is assigned to the results of that test (in terms of Popper's analogy, it depends upon the jury's verdict and the judge's sentence). In any event, the theory always sustains some impact from each test of fit between hypothesis and finding, and in a revised form it may then be used as the source of a new hypothesis, thus beginning a new cycle in the scientific process.

It is important to add that each test, as just described, examines the theoretically deduced hypothesis not in its unique *conceptual* form, but in only one of its many possible inter-

2. See Kaplan (1964:311-322) for discussion of "correspondence," "coherence," and "pragmatic" norms governing the validation of theories.

3. As Merton aptly puts it, "Appropriately investigated, the exception can improve the rule" (1959:xxxii).

4. See Popper (1961:87), Kuhn (1964:*passim*), and Greer (1969:109-25, esp.118).

5. Kaplan stresses the relative nature of theory confirmation: "The acceptability of a theory will in any case be a matter of degree — more or less weight will be assigned to it, and it will always have a more or less limited range of justified application" (1964:312).

preted forms, and at only one of the indefinitely large number of times and places that it could be tested. Each test of a hypothesis is, in short, a sample drawn from the universe of possible tests, and as with any sample, the question of its representativeness arises. The manner in which this question is handled typically involves *repeated* tests of the same hypothesis — differently interpreted at different times and places, sometimes by different researchers[6] — such that the evidence for or against the deduced conceptual hypothesis "accumulates," becomes "persuasive," and finally is "overwelming." Obviously different hypotheses deduced from the same theory will require different accumulations of tests in order to become fully accepted or fully rejected, depending on the importance of the hypothesis to the theory, the amount of support that has already been built up for the theory and for the hypothesis itself, etc.[7]

In almost all cases, however, several tests of a given hypothesis are required. Ordinarily, once a theory has been formulated to cover a given substantive area, research on it proceeds as just outlined; that is, through comparing deduced hypotheses with empirical generalizations designed to test them, and then incorporating the results of each test into the theory. But Merton has pointed out that research on one theoretically derived hypothe-

6. One kind of error ("response error") in empirical generalizations springs from the variability that inheres in the observables themselves. We seek to minimize this error by improving interpretative, sampling, measurement, and other related procedures. But a second kind of error ("observer error") springs from variability in researchers' applications of scientific methods. The argument that studies should be replicated, especially by different researchers, seems to address this second kind of error.

7. See Stinchcombe (1968:18-20) for a similar discussion of "multiple tests of theories" in which Durkheim's *Suicide* is used as an illustration. Blalock also discusses the desirability of overidentifying a mathematized hypothesis: When we "have more empirical information than necessary to estimate the coefficients, (then) the equations in question would be said to be 'overidentified.' A highly overidentified system that has successfully resisted elimination by implying numerous correct predictions can therefore be considered more adequately tested than one that is just barely overidentified" (1969:68, 69). See also Webb, *et al.* (1966:3-5).

sis sometimes yields empirical generalizations that are relevant to a quite different hypothesis or theory. Merton discusses this occurrence:

> Fruitful empirical research not only tests theoretically derived hypotheses; it also originates new hypotheses. This might be termed the "serendipity" component of research, i.e., the discovery, by chance or sagacity, of valid results which were not sought for.
>
> The serendipity pattern refers to the fairly common experience of observing an *unanticipated, anomalous and strategic* datum which becomes the occasion for developing a new theory or for extending a different theory (1957:103,104).

It would appear that in this description Merton is referring to the eventuality — indicated in Figure 1 by the *direct* transformation of "empirical generalizations" into "theories" — that such generalizations, although deliberately constructed for purposes of testing hypotheses previously deduced from a theory, can sometimes lead more directly, and unexpectedly, to new theoretical statements.

But the concept "serendipity" may usefully be extended literally to include *all* research "results" — that is, more than observing a datum that occasions a new theory — and it may also be given greater specificity by distinguishing various kinds of serendipity. Figure 1, together with my earlier comments regarding the indispensable role of trials (both imaginary and actual) in the scientific process, seems to suggest two principles for accomplishing this extension and specification. Thus, it may be assumed that: (1) each of the several information components, methodological controls, and information transformations constitute a point at which "valid results which were not sought for" can appear; and (2) each trial — whether imaginary or actual — constitutes an occasion for such appearance. The social causes and social consequences that (1) differentiate the appearance of serendipity at one point in the scientific process from its appearance at another point, and that (2) differentiate

the appearance of serendipity during one trial from its appearance during another trial, would seem potentially fruitful areas
for investigation.

Chapter Six

THEORIES

Theories

Having briefly discussed some relationships among the elements shown in Figure 1, let us return for a closer look at theories[1] in particular, since they constitute the most inclusive information component of the scientific process and since it may be argued that theorizing has an especially human quality:

> Whether or not theory formation is the most important and distinctive scientific activity, in one sense of the term "theory" this activity might well be regarded as the most important and distinctive for human beings. In this sense it stands for the symbolic dimension of experience, as opposed to the apprehension of brute fact . . . to engage in theorizing means not just to learn by experience but to take thought about what is there to be learned (Kaplan 1964:294).

I propose here to examine the *structure* of theories, and then to discuss various explanatory-predictive *strategies* that, by vir-

---

1. The difference between a theory and a model may be mentioned in passing, as summed up by Kaplan: "In general, we learn something about the subject-matter *from* the theory, but not by investigating properties *of* the theory (as we would with a model). The theory *states* that the subject-matter has a certain structure, but the theory does not therefore necessarily *exhibit* that structure in itself (as does a model)" (1964:264-265). See Braithwaite (1960:esp. 90-93), and Wartofsky (1968:143-146, and 280-287) for similar views.The term "theory," as used throughout the present essay, includes what is sometimes referred to as "theory-sketch."

tue of this structure, are open to the theoretically oriented scientist. Following that, I will discuss some dimensions in which the *phenomenal referents* of theories may vary, and some ways that the *concepts* or terms of theories may vary.

The Structure of Theories

As indicated above, theories have two functions in the scientific process: they *explain* empirical generalizations that are already known (that is, they summarize the past of a science), and they *predict* empirical generalizations that are still unknown (that is, they guide the future of a science). And not only do confirmed predictions increase our confidence in theoretic explanations,[2] but the reverse is also true: satisfactory explanations increase our confidence in theoretic predictions. Thus each builds confidence in the other and the two together build confidence in the theory itself.

This interaction between the past and future implications of theories seems directly to serve the paramount goal of all science: to identify Necessity in nature. That is, in the sciences we want to know not only how things "have worked" in the past, not only how things "will work" in the future, but both[3] — and more than that, we want to know both in one statement. In short, we want to know how things "*must* work," since only an expression of Necessity[4] can give the single, united

2. Sheffler notes that "making predictions is part of one way of confirming the existence of explanations" (1960:280), but argues for the equal centrality of both in science.

3. Reference to the "present" is omitted, since the infinitesmally small instant to which it ultimately refers may be considered either part of the "past" or the "future," depending on one's chief interest.

4. Bohm notes that we interpret "the constancy of certain relationships inside a wide variety of transformations and changes" as "signifying that such relationships are *necessary,* in the sense that they could not be otherwise, because they are inherent and essential aspects of what things are" (1961:1). Wartofsky says, still more strongly, "The claim we tend to make for a law of nature is that it holds independently of whether anyone knows it or not,

image of past and future that we seek. For a sociological example, we do not want only to understand social stratification in ancient societies, nor do we want only to understand it in present or only in future societies. Rather, we want to understand social stratification as such, wherever and whenever it might appear.

Certainly, it is no inconsiderable task to understand past phenomena alone or future phenomena alone; but if one pursues each understanding separately, the result is likely to be two quite different understandings: the past, understood "on its own terms," and the future, understood "on its own terms." The task is magnified enormously when, in the sciences, we insist on possessing both in one understanding. The task is so magnified, indeed, as to become literally impossible because apparently it is not given to man to know the future in the sense that we can know the past; we can only guess (predict) the future. Any newly discovered fact may nullify our prediction, thus reducing the scope of our understanding to the past alone (at best), and thereby nullifying the presumption that we understand Necessity in the world.

Nevertheless, in full recognition of the impossibility of success, we irresistibly pursue the understanding of Necessity, chiefly through the past-future, explanatory-predictive references of theory. Through this double reference, we continually and simultaneously ask the two-fold approximation to the Necessity question: Will what we have discovered to be true of the past continue to be true of the future? Will what we discover to be true of the future turn out to have been true also of the past?

---

and even independently of whether it is possible to know it . . . . We might say, even if there never was a falling body, and never will be, in fact; still, if there were, it would fall in accordance with Galileo's law . . ." (1968:251). In the same vein, Kaplan refers to a theory as "more than a synopsis of the moves that have been played in the game of nature, it also sets forth some idea of the rules of the game by which the moves become intelligible" (1964:-302). See also Quine (1967).

If this simultaneously backward and forward reach of theory may be considered the primary manifestation of the way science pursues Necessity, two general rules for the internal structuring of theory seem to serve as the primary instruments of this pursuit: the rules of logical deduction, and the rules of causality (including, in the latter, the rules of chance).[5] By this I mean that, for brief example, we tend to accept as true the statement that "Socrates is mortal" (Socrates will die) if: (1) it is a logical deduction from previously accepted premises, such as, "All men are mortal" and "Socrates is a man"; or (2) it expresses a causal result of convergent antecedents, such as the development of political relationships between Socrates and the court of Athens, and of metabolic relationships within Socrates' body.[6] Perhaps we accept the two kinds of statements on differ-

5. I shall not attempt to define causality here, except to say that I prefer definitions that involve notions of regular, asymmetrical action at a vanishing distance in time and space, as in Feigl (1953:408-418), Braithwaite (1960:-308-311) and Nagel (1961:74). The inadequacy of causality rules to express modern physics theories, especially regarding elementary particles, must be acknowledged. However, in theories of more macrophenomena, the rules of causality still seem powerful means for seeking Necessity in nature. For a discussion of the place of chance, as well as causality, in scientific theory, see Bohm: "The processes taking place in nature have been found to satisfy laws that are more general than those of causality. For these processes may also satisfy laws of chance . . . , and also laws which deal with the relationships between causality and chance" (1961:3, see also 20-32, 140-143). In one interpretation (which I prefer), "chance" refers not to the absolute absence of causation, but to the presence of many small, unknown causes, such as may be said to determine whether a given fair coin lands with its head or tail uppermost on a given toss. For a discussion of several meanings of "chance" (including this one), see Nagel (1961:324-335); and for a discussion of randomness, see Stinchcombe (1968: 23-24).

6. It should be noted that Nagel holds that "not all laws of nature are causal," and discusses five other (including subtypes) "types of laws that are used as explanatory premises in various sciences" (1961:75-78). However, I believe it may be argued that all such types of laws, even though they do not themselves specify causation, are explainable by (because deducible from) causal laws and therefore could be reformulated in causal (although more cumbersome) terms. That the former laws are not expressed in causal terms

ent intuitive bases: logical deduction seems to answer "why" a given phenomenon exists (it "follows"), while causality answers "how" it exists (it "results"). But in any case, the strong, culturally engendered feeling that we can "understand" something when the rules of logic or causality are adhered to in statements purporting to explain it may account for the internal structure of scientific theories. That is, scientific theories may be described as sets of propositions organized into logical deductive systems and into causal systems, depending on whether, and at what points, they rely for the imputation of Necessity chiefly on the rules of logic or of causality.

Kaplan distinguishes two types of theory that seem to correspond to this scientific reliance on the rules of logic and of causality as two prime aspects of the internal structure of theories. He calls one structure "hierarchical" or "deductive," apparently because the connection between the explanans (the set of statements that explain) and the explanandum (the statements describing the thing that is to be explained) is a logically deductive one:

> A hierarchical theory is one whose component laws are presented as deductions from a small set of basic principles. A law is explained by the demonstration that it is a logical consequence of these principles, and a fact that explained when it is shown to follow from these together with certain initial conditions (1964:298).

---

seems therefore to be a matter of notation and style rather than substance. Thus, it would appear that laws stating "an invariable concomitance of determinate properties in every object that is of a certain kind" (Nagel 1961:75-76) — for example, the concomitance of density and hardness in minerals — and laws that state a "functional dependence (in the mathematical sense of 'function') between two or more variable magnitudes associated with stated properties or processes" (Nagel 1961:77) — for example, the dependence of pressure, temperature and volume in gases — now are deducible from, and formulable in terms of, statistical causal laws at the molecular and atomic level.

The examples Kaplan gives of hierarchical theory are the theory of relativity in physics, Mendelian genetic theory, and Keynesian economic theory. Kaplan calls a second structure (more familiar in sociology) "concatenated" or "patterned":

> A *concatenated* theory is one whose component laws enter into a network of relations so as to constitute an identifiable configuration or pattern. Most typically, they converge on some central point, each specifying one of the factors which plays a part in the phenomenon which the theory is to explain (it has therefore been called a theory of the "factor type," as contrasted with the "law type" . . . .) This is especially likely to be true of a theory consisting of tendency statements, which attain closure only in their joint application (1964:298).

The examples given of concatenated theories are the "big bang" theory in cosmology, the theory of biological evolution, and the psychoanalytic theory of neuroses. In such theories, it would seem that the connection between the explanandum or "central point" and the explanans or "component laws" is more likely to be causal[7] than deductive.

Zetterberg lends more detail to this basic structural dichotomy by listing six "currently used formats" for ordering sociological propositions; they are: inventory of determinants, inventory of results, chain pattern of propositions, matrixes of propositions, axiomatic format with definitional reduction, and axiomatic format with propositional reduction (1963:26-34).[8] It would appear that the first four formats are ways that a causally structured theory (or, in Kaplan's terms, a concatenated the-

---

7. Kaplan indicates that the connection in the "pattern model" of explanation "may be of various different sorts: causal, purposive, mathematical, and perhaps other basic types" (1964:334), but it may be argued that "purpose" is a variety of "cause," and that all of the examples he gives of concatenated theories express causal relations, even though these are now highly mathematized in the case of the "big bang" theory in cosmology.

8. See Blalock (1969:35-47) for further discussion of the first three of these.

ory) may be presented, while the last two formats are ways that a logically structured theory (or, in Kaplan's terms, a hierarchical theory) may be presented.[9]

Kaplan emphasizes that the two types of theory do not constitute "two kinds of explanation . . . but . . . two different reconstructions of explanation (different at least in formulation if not in substance), and . . . both may serve a useful purpose in methodology" (1964:332-333). In simplest form, Kaplan argues that ultimately there is but one kind of explanation: deductive. Thus, although the concatenated or pattern model theory serves most usefully during the early stages of theory formation, even then it must be reducible to the hierarchical or deductive model that is characteristic of more mature theories: "Fitting something into a pattern has explanatory force insofar as thereby we are enabled to show how what is being explained can be deduced from more general considerations" (1964:338). That is, the hypothesis that something fits into a given place in a given pattern is a deductive one, as is the higher-order hypothesis that the pattern itself fits into some larger pattern. Hempel presents a similar argument, identifying causal explanation as a special and often inferior case of deductive explanation. First, he defines "explanation":

> We divide an explanation into two major constituents, the *explanandum* and the *explanans*. By the explanandum, we understand the sentence describing the phenomenon to be explained (not that phenomenon itself); by the explanans the class of those sentences which are adduced to account for the phenomenon . . . . (the) explanans falls into two subclasses; one of these contains certain sentences C_1, C_2, . . . , C_k which state specific antecedent conditions; the other is a set of sentences L_1, L_2, . . . , L_r which represent general laws (1965:247).

9. The same underlying distinction between logically and causally structured theories may also play a part in Glaser's and Strauss' contrast between "logico-deductive theory" and "grounded theory" (1967).

Hempel then describes "deductive-nomological explanation, or D-N explanation for short" as showing that: "Given the particular circumstances (conditions, in the preceding quotation) and the laws in question, the occurrence of the phenomenon *was to be expected;* and it is in this sense that the explanation enables us to *understand why* the phenomenon occurred. In a D-N explanation, then, the explanandum is a logical consequence of the explanans" (1965:337). Now consider causal explanation:

> In the context of explanation, a "cause" must be allowed to be a more or less complex set of circumstances and events, which might be described by a set of statements C_1, C_2, . . . , C_k. . . . Thus the causal explanation implicitly claims that there are general laws — let us say, L_1, L_2, . . . ,L_k — in virtue of which the occurrence of the causal antecedents mentioned in C_1, C_2, . . . , C_k is a sufficient condition for the occurrence of the explanandum event . . . . causal explanation is, at least implicitly, deductive-nomological (1965:-348-49).

Thus, at this point[10] Hempel seems to identify as "causal" an explanation that makes explicit reference to the first subclass of the explanans (antecedent conditions) while making only implicit reference to the second subclass (general laws). But when an explanation makes equally explicit reference to both subclasses of its explanans, it becomes for Hempel "a truly general law" (1965:348), and presumably, deductive-nomological rather than merely causal.

Hempel has also distinguished "statistical explanation" (especially familiar to sociologists, and discussed by Costner and [Leik 1964] and [Blalock 1968:155-159]) from strictly "de-

10. In the same discussion, Hempel also suggests that causal explanations may leave "the relevant antecedent conditions (as well as) the requisite explanatory laws indefinite" (1965:349). But it would seem that an explanation whose explanans is *wholly* indefinite (and equally so in both of its subclasses) can be neither an explanation nor even a "sketch" for one.

ductive-nomological" explanation, while stressing the common qualities of both:

> Explanation based on . . . probabilistic laws I will call *probabilistic explanations*. Because of the statistical character of the laws it invokes, a probabilistic explanation shows only that, in view of the specified laws and particular circumstances, the phenomenon to be explained was to be expected with more or less high probability; whereas a deductive explanation shows that, given the truth of the explanatory information, the occurrence of the phenomenon in question follows with deductive certainty.
>
> But deductive and probabilistic explanations agree in their essential reliance on covering laws; both explain a given phenomenon by showing that it occurs in conformance with such laws. I think that this is indeed a common characteristic of all scientific explanations. . . . (1967:84).[11]

It would seem that statistical explanations can take either form described by Kaplan — concatenated or hierarchical — and that they are distinguishable by the content of their constituent propositions and laws rather than by the form in which the latter are arranged. But whether statistical or deterministic in content, hierarchically arranged theories have received the greater attention in the philosophy of science. Nagel, for example, says, "Ever since Aristotle analyzed the structure of what he believed to be the ideal of science, the view that scientific explanations must always be ordered in the form of a logical deduction has had wide acceptance" (1961:29). And Braithwaite says:

> A scientific theory is a deductive system (consisting) of a set of propositions (to be called the *initial propositions*) from which all the other propositions (to be called the *deduced propositions*) follow according to logical principles.[12]

11. See also Hempel 1965:376-412.
12. For similar definitions of "theory," see Nagel (1961:90ff.), Popper (1961:59ff), Bergmann (1958:31-32), Merton (1967:39), Zetterberg (1954:10), and Blalock (1969:2).

The propositions in a deductive system may be considered as being arranged in an order of levels, the hypotheses at the highest level being those which occur only as premises in the system, those at the lowest level being those which occur only as conclusions in the system, and those at intermediate levels being those which occur as conclusions of deductions from higher-level hypotheses and which serve as premises for deductions to lower-level hypotheses (1960:22,12).

Thus, in the deductive form of scientific theory, once the initial propositions have been selected, the rules of logic become the sole determinants of the relation of one proposition to another. Because these rules are relatively simple, unambiguous, and very well understood (and are human creations, besides), they can be used (1) to assert the logical necessity of propositions for which empirical research can assert only empirical truth (that is, to explain); and (2) to locate places in the theory where logically necessary propositions are absent and to specify the characteristics that such propositions, if they existed, must have (that is, to predict). As Zetterberg puts it, "An axiomatic schema ... makes visible *all* ideas implicit in *some* given ideas. . . . It forces (the theorist) to spell out his assumptions, to make explicit his deductions and it will remind him of any bypassed implications" (1963:34, see also 73-78).

However, although logic is the sole determinant (in a deductive theory) of the relation of one proposition to another, it cannot be the sole determinant of whether a given proposition is in a theory at all, because:

There must be many theoretical systems with a logical structure very similar to the one which at any particular time is the accepted system of empirical science. This situation is sometimes described by saying that there are a great many — presumably an infinite number — of "logically possible worlds." Yet the system called "empirical science" is intended to represent only *one* world: the "real world" or the "world of our experience" . . . (Popper, 1961:39).

It is just this problem of identifying the empirically true propositions out of all logically possible propositions[13] that gives observation its pivotal role in science. " 'Experience,' on this view, appears as a distinctive method whereby one theoretical system may be distinguished from others" (Popper 1961:39).[14] Insofar as a theoretical system has not been fully tested against experience, however, it must be considered open at all levels; at the highest, most general level to new and more broadly explanatory inductions; in the middle to new propositions and rearrangement of old ones;[15] and at the bottom to new and more precisely predictive hypotheses. Indeed, most of what is meant by the "progress" of science involves predicting and testing new empirical observations, rearranging propositions, and inventing and examining new "postulates," "axioms," or "initial propositions" that supersede (by logically incorporating rather than by displacing) old ones. Thus, whatever is thought to be "ultimate" at either end of a theory at a particular moment in its history may, at the very next moment, be considered only intermediate.[16] It therefore seems most reasonable to think of both the highest-order initial propositions and the lowest-order de-

13. See Blalock (1969:48-75, esp. 64).

14. "It is just because the propositions . . . investigated by the empirical sciences can be denied without logical absurdity that observational evidence is required to support them" (Nagel 1961:21). And Carnap writes: "Consider the law: 'When iron is heated, it expands.' Another law says: 'When iron is heated, it contracts.' There is no logical inconsistency in this second law. From the standpoint of pure logic, it is no more invalid than the first law. The first law is accepted, rather than the second, only because it describes a regularity *observed in nature*" (1966:199).

15. As Zetterberg points out: "There is no inherent difference between postulates and theorems. The postulates are in no respect more "basic," "granted," or "self-evident" than the theorems" (1954:20). Bergmann agrees: "To call a law either an axiom or a theorem is not to say anything about the law itself; it merely says something about its position in a theory" (1957:32). Blalock offers two rules for distinguishing axioms and theorems (1969:10-26, esp. 18).

16. See Kaplan's discussion of the "openness" of explanations (1964:-351-356).

duced propositions and empirical hypotheses of any theory as
"initial" or "of low order" *within the limits of present thinking
and knowledge:* that is, not absolutely but only relatively and
temporarily "initial" or "of low order." This implies that theoretic work in sociology (or in any science) can take the form of
inducing more fundamental initial propositions as well as deducing more detailed hypotheses — that is, "generalizing" as
well as "specifying" theory. [17] Referring to the former process,
Popper says:

The various ideas and hypotheses [of a science] might be visualized

17. Barton's discussion of the concept of property-space is directly relevant to both processes, although this relevance may not be immediately clear,
owing, I think to the strong visual ambiguity that is involved when one says
a given concept or proposition is more "basic," "fundamental," "primitive,"
or "initial" than another. The visual problem is whether the more basic
concept should be visualized as "lower" than the other, "underlying" it, and
from which the latter "rises"; or whether the more basic concept should be
visualized as "higher" than the other, and from which the other "descends."
The latter image, wherein the most "basic" concepts or propositions are
"higher" and other concepts are propositions in the theory descend from
them by logical deduction, seems more conventional in the philosophy of
science literature. (See Braithwaite 1960:21 – 23.) Thus an "hypothesis" is
literally an *under* thesis deduced (dependent) from the conjunction of higher
theses. Barton, however, adopts the reverse image (common enough in depict-
ing genealogical, phylogenetic, and geological descent), and defines substruction as "the procedure of finding, for a given set of types, the property space
in which they are located and the reduction which has implicitly been used
in their formation" (1955:50). In other words, Barton refers to the search for
more basic, conventionally, "higher," dimensions as *sub*struction. By implication then, "*super*struction" (my own term, not Barton's) of the property
space would correspond to the procedure of finding, for a given general
property space, the set of more specific, conventionally "lower," types that
is located there. (Barton refers to one variety of "superstruction" as "reduction" primarily because the number of types found in a given property-space
is here reduced from what it might be if the precision available in each
dimension of the property-space were used to the fullest extent.) However,
once the ambiguous directional implications of "sub-" and "super-" struction
(and "reduction") are resolved, it seems clear that they refer to logical induction and deduction, respectively. Zetterberg refers to what Barton would call
property-space "reduction" as "extracting the ordinary propositions from
theoretical ones" and "decomposing terms," and to what Barton would call

as particles suspended in a fluid. Testable science is the precipitation of these particles at the bottom of the vessel: they settle down in layers (of universality). The thickness of the deposit grows with the number of these layers, every new layer corresponding to a theory more universal than those beneath it (1961:277-278).

Explanatory-Predictive Strategies

It follows, from the different kinds of internal structures of theories tending to give scientific satisfaction, that when a scientist wishes to explain or predict a given phenomenon (more correctly, of course, a given empirical generalization about that phenomenon), he can adopt differing strategies.[18] The two causal strategies[19] include the search for (a) causes of the phenomenon; and for (b) effects of the phenomenon. Durkheim indicated both of these as follows: "When, then, the explanation of a social phenomenon is undertaken, we must seek separately the efficient cause which produces it and the function it fulfills" (1964:95). Two other strategies may be called *compositional*, since they include the search for (a) component entities, processes or properties (parts of the phenomenon); and for (b) larger "background" wholes of which the phenomenon is itself

---

property-space "substruction" as "subsuming" one term under another (1963:21-25).

18. Compare this discussion with Nagel's wherein deductive, probabilistic, functional or teleological, and genetic explanations are discussed (1961:-20-26). My own view classifies the latter three together as variants of the causal (a) strategy, and the first as a classificatory strategy. For an exposition of realist, nominalist, and conventionalist views of the nature of explanation, see Wartofsky (1968:257-276).

19. See Stinchcombe (1968:33-37) for discussion of methods for observing covariation, causal direction, and nonspuriousness; and also for discussion of several causal explanations currently in use by sociologists (1968:57-130). For discussions of path or dependence analysis in evaluating multivariable causal theories, see Duncan (1966 and 1969), Boudon (1968), Land (1969), and Heise (1969).

a part. Durkheim also indicated these strategies, but somewhat more implicitly: "To have a satisfactory understanding of [social life], it is necessary to show how the phenomena comprising it combine in such a way as to put society in harmony with itself and with the environment external to it" (1964:97).

Taking the point of view of modern physics, Bohm also describes the compositional strategies, first (a):

> We have considered how experiments have shown the existence of level within level of smaller and smaller kinds of entities, each of which helps to constitute the substructure of the entities above it in size, and each of which helps to explain . . . the qualities of the entities above it. . . .

Then (b)

> But now we must take into account the fact that the basic qualities and properties of each kind of entity depend not only on their substructures but also on what is happening in their general background (1961:138; see also p. 10).

And in part, Kaplan's discussion of the "pattern model" of explanation also describes the compositional (b) strategy: "Something is explained when it is so related to a set of other elements that together they constitute a unified system. We understand something by identifying it as a specific part in an organized whole" (1964:333).

Both compositional strategies may be viewed as subtypes of the causal strategies:[20] compositional (a) seeks certain *endoge-*

---

20. Bohm points out that at least in physics, the study of "properties of things" (including properties that permit one thing to combine with another — that is properties revealed by the compositional strategy referred to above) rests on the study of causes of those things: "Causal connections exist which permit the prediction of the new properties that things develop after they have undergone certain processes, treatments, reactions, etc." (1961:13), and "It becomes possible by studying the laws of the atomic motions to make many kinds of approximate predictions concerning the laws and properties of things at the large-scale level and in this way to improve

nous causes and effects, while compositional (b) seeks certain *exogenous* causes and effects).

To illustrate the above strategies, suppose one wanted to explain and predict bureaucracy as a form of social organization.[21] The causal (a) strategy might show bureaucracy to be an outcome of a money economy, the state, increase and diversification of administrative tasks, and so on; or an outcome of the problems of succession that arise, for instance, when a charismatic leader grows feeble and dies. The causal (b) strategy might emphasize phenomena such as the spread of universalistic criteria of recruitment in the society as a whole; growing dominance of an impersonal, dispassionate, attitude toward other persons; and so on. The compositional (a) strategy might yield an inventory showing that bureaucracy consists of hierarchical organization of officials, appointed on the basis of technical qualifications alone, each having a specified sphere of competence and responsibility, strictly governed by procedural rules, and so on. The compositional (b) strategy might yield another inventory showing bureaucracy to be a component part or property of more inclusive social entities, such as nations, voluntary associations, labor unions, political parties, etc.

The logico-deductive or hierarchical structural type of theories is best reflected in a third strategy which may be called the *classificatory* strategy. Here the scientist seeks to locate the phenomenon of interest in a taxonomic scheme and to deduce, from its position there, more information than is directly known about the phenomenon itself. Using the bureaucracy example again, the classificatory strategy would yield statements detailing taxonomic relationships between bureaucracy and other forms of social organization (families, cliques, crowds, teams, etc.) from which one might conclude that bureaucracy is a special case of some of the factors operating in

our understanding and control of the large-scale level" (1961:145).

21. The following illustration is based roughly on Max Weber's discussions (1946:204-214; 1947:329-341, 363-386).

all these latter. Blalock illustrates the approach that the classificatory strategy implies in explaining the low incidence of suicide in Spain: If we grant the proposition that "the suicide rate varies with the incidence of Protestantism," and if Spain can be shown to belong to "the set of all nations having incidences of Protestantism defined as 'low' " then Blalock says, "we have 'explained' a property of Spain by showing that Spain also belongs to, or is an element of, another class . . . of nations for which all members have a given property (e.g., low suicide rates)" (1969:143).

Nagel discusses the classificatory strategy as most useful in the primitive stages of a science:

> The development of comprehensive theoretical systems seems to be possible only after a preliminary classification of kinds [of phenomena that are embraced by the science in question] has been achieved, and the history of science repeatedly confirms the view that the noting and mutual ordering of various kinds — a stage of inquiry often called "natural history" — is a prerequisite for the discovery of more commonly recognized types of laws and for the construction of far-reaching theories. . . When a system of inclusion between kinds is achieved, it is possible to explain (even if only in a crude fashion) why some individual thing is a member of a specified kind by showing that the individual is a member of a subordinate kind (for example, the family pet is a mammal because it is a cat and cats are mammals). Such explanations are obviously far removed from the sort of explanations to which the modern theoretical sciences have accustomed us; nevertheless, they are early steps on the road which leads to the latter (1961:31,n.2).[22]

The classificatory strategy, when used during the early history of a science, is likely to be primitive because the several causal and compositional elements of which it is comprised may not yet have been systematically sorted out and therefore not

22. Bohm also locates the classificatory strategy early in the history of a science (1961:15).

yet systematically put together. The primitive classificatory strategy is therefore a "mix" of generally known ingredients and unknown quantities and sequences.[23] In Nagel's example, one does not yet have adequate causal and/or compositional explanations for why there are mammals, why there are cats, and why there are family pets. However, a classificatory strategy may also appear during the more mature history of a science, when it can become a shorthand notation[24] for a known and logically arranged combination of causal and compositional explanatory elements.[25] The modern versions of the periodic table of elements, the color-brightness diagrams of stellar populations, and the phylogenetic ordering of living things serve to illustrate this. When the classificatory strategy is used in this latter fashion, it seems to have at least two advantages: (1) it advances explanatory parsimony — insofar as the same kinds of causes, effects, components and/or memberships may be attributed to a variety of phenomena; and (2) — as Blalock's example shows — it provides a ready source from which new hypotheses may be deduced about the phenomenon in question — insofar as phenomena known to share similar components may be tentatively expected to share similar memberships, causes, and/or effects.[26]

23. See Zetterberg's discussion of "the taxonomical approach" (1963:5-8), and Kaplan (1964:50-53).

24. See Kaplan (1964:49) regarding notational and substantive concepts.

25. See Durkheim's distinction between "morphological" and "aetiological" classifications (1951:145-148, 277-278). These seem to correspond to what I refer to here as primitive and mature versions of the classificatory strategy.

26. Campbell makes essentially this point regarding the utility of the classification strategy: "There is often in practical diagnostic procedures an iteration between similarity [of attributes of different phenomena] and common fate [covariability in time of different phenomena] criteria in which an observed similarity dimension may provide an hypothesized grouping which is then tested for intragroup homogeneity on various dimensions of common fate" (1958:21). Needless to say, certain dangers of error, and especially of error perpetuation, are also associated with the classification strategy. See Kuhn (1964,esp. 91-109).

To summarize the strategies discussed above, suppose one wished to explain a phenomenon, Y. One could adopt a strategy leading to statements in any or all of the following forms:

Causal (a): Y is caused by such-and-such antecedents.

Causal (b): Y causes such-and-such consequences.

Compositional (a): Y is composed of such-and-such properties, entities, or processes.

Compositional (b): Y is a component of such-and-such properties, entities, or processes.

Classificatory: Y can be located in a particular class of such-and-such taxonomy.

This general discussion of types of deductive strategies should make clear why "descriptive" and "explanatory" studies are so highly interdependent in scientific work as a whole. Often when we say a study is "descriptive," we mean it manifests a compositional strategy, in which the parts or properties of the subject phenomenon and/or the larger wholes of which it is a part are catalogued.[27] Similarly, when a study is called "explanatory," we usually mean it follows one or both causal strategies and sets forth the causes and/or effects of the phenomenon. But it would seem that a fully satisfactory explanation of any phenomenon requires both strategies, in both aspects of each.

Scope

Here I mean the property space described by two dimensions of theories: the substantive range of reference, and the spatiotemporal range of reference contained in their explananda.[28] To illustrate variability in substantive range, consider that a

---

27. Not always, since some studies are (charitably) called "descriptive" because they simply list causal and compositional findings in unsystematic, seemingly unaware, ways. For a discussion of "descriptive research and hypothesis testing," see Dubin (1969:6, 226-229).

28. Kaplan defines "range" and "scope" as different rather than synony-

theory may seek to explain only bureaucracy, or only reference groups, or only social mobility, or only urbanization, etc., rather than an entire social system of which reference groups, bureaucracy, etc., may be parts or properties or processes. As a result, one may say that the substantive range of explananda in the former is narrower than in the latter. To illustrate variability in spatiotemporal range, consider that a theory may seek to explain only bureaucracy in nineteenth century Germany, in contrast with explaining bureaucracy whenever or wherever it may be found. Similarly, a theory may seek to explain only the American social system in the twentieth century, in contrast with explaining any social system at any time and place.

Ultimately, we seek verified theories that have maximum scope in both the substantive and the spatiotemporal sense, since, if they are indeed verified theories, all theories of lesser substantive or spatiotemporal scope can be deduced from them and therefore explained by them. The very wide scope of the atomic theory of matter and of relativity theory (as compared with, say, Boyle's Law and Newtonian mechanics) is obviously one of their strongest features. It has been pointed out, however, that useful theories of great scope (in either sense) are more apt to be induced from prior theories of lesser scope than to spring full-blown from abstract speculation. Although Popper denies the role of logical induction in this process, his opinion is clearly relevent here:

The question may be raised: "Why not invent theories of the highest

---

mous extensions. In briefest form, it would appear that Kaplan applies the term "range" to explanantes or independent variables, and the term "scope" to explananda or dependent variables (1964:94-95, but see 299-300 for an apparently different usage of "range," and for usage of "explanatory shell" as apparently synonymous with "scope"). Popper's usage of "range" is different still: "The 'range' which a statement allows to reality is, as it were, the amount of 'free play' (or the degree of freedom) which it allows to reality. Range and empirical content are converse (or complementary) concepts" (1961:124).

level of universality straight away? Why wait for this quasi-inductive evolution?". . . Those theories which are on too high a level of universality, as it were (that is, too far removed from the level reached by the testable science of the day) give rise, perhaps, to a "metaphysical system" . . . . A link with the science of the day is as a rule established only by those theories which are proposed in an attempt to meet the current problem situation (1961:277).

And Merton says, with specific relevance to sociological theory:

Some sociologists still write as though they expect, here and now, formulation of *the* general sociological theory broad enough to encompass the vast ranges of precisely observed details of social behavior, organization, and change and fruitful enough to direct the attention of research workers to a flow of problems for empirical research. This I take to be a premature and apocalyptic belief. We are not ready. Not enough preparatory work has been done (1967:45).

But, Merton continues, dangers beset sociology at both extremes of substantive (and presumably, also spatiotemporal) scope:

To concentrate entirely on special theories is to risk emerging with specific hypotheses that account for limited aspects of social behavior, organization and change but that remain mutually inconsistent.

To concentrate entirely on a master conceptual scheme for deriving all subsidiary theories is to risk producing twentieth-century sociological equivalents of the large philosophical systems of the past, with all their varied suggestiveness, their archetectonic splendor, and their scientific sterility (1967:51).

The surest path, according to Merton, leads from special theories to general theories, rather than the reverse:[29]

We sociologists can look instead toward progressively comprehensive sociological theory which, instead of proceeding from the head of one man, gradually consolidates theories of the middle range, so

29. See Blalock (1969:142) for a similar view.

that these become special cases of more general formulations (1967:51).

Level of Abstraction

Whereas "scope" measures the substantive and spatiotemporal extensions of that part of the universe coming within a given theory's purview, "level of abstraction" measures the closeness of that theory's concepts to actual observations.[30] When a theory is cast at a low level of abstraction, it is more nearly an already interpreted set of "test hypotheses," in contrast with a theory that is cast at a high level of abstraction, whose terms are more ideational, more distant from actual observations, and whose interpretation is highly problematic. Although, as Blalock says: "A deductively formulated theory cannot be tested directly without the aid of an auxiliary theory consisting of assumptions linking at least some of the theoretical variables with operational procedures" (1969:151), the nature of such operationized "auxiliary theory" will vary, depending on the main theory's level of abstraction. Again in Blalock's terms:

> The higher the level of abstraction . . . the more difficult it will be to link measured indicators to these abstract concepts. Also, the wider the variety of situations to which the theory applies, the greater one's choice of indicators and, perhaps, the greater the reliance that should be placed on the use of multiple indicators (1969:152).

It seems obvious that scope and level of abstraction are related dimensions of theories: the higher the level of abstraction, the wider the scope. For example, to raise the level of abstraction from "number of census occupations" to "division

30. Kaplan refers to the "abstractness" of a theory as "the length of the reduction chain connecting the theoretical terms into observable ones" (1964:301).

of labor" clearly implies a broader substantive and spatiotemporal range within which relevant observations may be found. But at this point, two important complications in the relationship between scope and level of abstraction must be noted.

First, the positive relationship of scope to level of abstraction does not seem to be mutual; although an increase in level of abstraction implies an increase in scope, an increase in scope does not necessarily imply an increase in level of abstraction. For example, to raise the scope of a theory from reference groups to entire societies does not necessarily require any change in the abstraction of terms (although it may require adding some) employed to denote the theoretic explananda or explanantes. Indeed, one recommendation for theories of broad scope is that the same abstractions (concepts) apply throughout all substantive and spatiotemporal extensions.

Second, insofar as a change in level of abstraction implies a change in scope, the latter change is logically indefinite. By increasing the level of abstraction from "number of census occupations" to "division of labor" we know we broaden scope, but we do not know in what way or to what extent. Only empirical tests of hypotheses in different substantive and spatiotemporal spheres can indicate the nature of the change in scope that is implied in a change in level of abstraction.

Perhaps because of these complications in the relationship of scope and level of abstraction (which make for an appearance at times of logical dependence and at other times of logical independence), these two dimensions of theories are sometimes mixed indiscriminately. For example, although I referred above to Merton's distinction between "middle-range theories" and "total systems of theory" as pertaining to scope, his discussion seems to pertain to level of abstraction as well. Thus, on the one hand, Merton says: "Middle-range theories deal with delimited aspects of social phenomena. . . ." (1967:39); and "Our major task today is to develop special theories applicable to limited conceptual ranges — theories, for example, of deviant behavior, the unanticipated consequences of purposive action, social perception, reference groups, social control, the interdependence of social institutions" (1967:51). These descriptions of middle-range theory I take to refer to the scope dimension. But on the other hand, Merton says: "Middle-range theory is principally used in sociology to guide empirical inquiry. . . . Middle-range theory involves abstractions, of course, but they are close enough to observed data to be incorporated in propositions that permit empirical testing" (1967:39). And this I take to be a reference to the level-of-abstraction dimension.

In addition to having this apparent indistinctness, the term "middle-range" may be more vulnerable to criticism on its level-of-abstraction meaning than on its scope meaning, since the former may imply a derogation of the distinctive role of theories (induced, inherently "abstract," items of information) as compared with interpreted hypotheses or auxiliary theories (deduced, inherently "concrete" items of information). More specifically, insofar as "middle-range" implies operationalism, it is open to the same criticisms that have been leveled at the latter point of view.[31] As a result of this combination of ambiguous meaning and differential vulnerability between the two possible meanings, it is not surprising that theorists of the middle range have been, as Merton says, "stereotyped as mere nose-counters or mere fact-finders or as merely descriptive sociographers" (1967:53); that is, as advocating that propositions be cast only at low or middling levels of abstraction, regardless of their scope, rather than recognized as advocating propositions and theories cast at low or middling levels of scope, regardless of their abstraction. Insofar as the scope meaning of "theories of the middle range" is primary, such theories appear to be a subcategory within the information component "theories" shown in Figure 1. But insofar as the level of abstraction meaning is primary, middle-range theories might constitute an

31. See Hempel (1952:37-50).

information component intermediate between empirical generalizations and theories, on the one hand, and between theories and hypotheses, on the other.[32]

Parsimony

If one theory deals with a more complex explanandum than another theory, we should naturally expect the former to be more complex than the latter. But the requirement that even the former theory should nevertheless be "parsimonious" means that it should be *free of redundancy;* that is, it should be simple, relative to other possible theories accounting for the same explanandum. If the theory, in short, could do as well or better without a given element of form or content, that element is an

32. Zetterberg also seems ambiguous regarding the relation between scope and level of abstraction: First, he draws a distinction between propositions of high and low *"informative value"* (that is, between "theoretic" and "ordinary" propositions): "the higher the informative value of a proposition, the greater is the variety of events for which it can account" (1963:21). He gives the example (at the level of individual concepts) of "approval," "esteem," and "rank" as each having lower informative value than "evaluations" (1963:21-22). This appears to make Zetterberg's "informative value" the parallel of "level of abstraction," as the latter term is used in the present essay. Then he distinguishes researches that have high and low scope: "By 'scope' I mean the proportion of all possible sources of data which is represented in a given research." To illustrate, Zetterberg cites examples in which "the theory could claim plausibility only in a limited population [but] when the scope [of a given research] was enlarged the theory was disproved" (1963:52), as in the impact of the discovery of Australian black swans on the "theory" that "all swans are white" (1963:52). This appears to make Zetterberg's "scope" the parallel at least of "spatiotemporal scope" if not also of "substantive scope," as the latter terms are used in the present essay. However, Zetterberg does not discuss possible relations between "informative value" and "scope," and thus he too leaves this question open. Zetterberg does speak of "propositions" as having informative value, and of "researches" as having scope; and he speaks of informative value as referring to "events," and of scope as referring to "data." These distinctions, which are themselves unexplicated, do not seem to reduce the ambiguity. Mills is similarly ambiguous regarding level of abstraction and scope when he distinguishes "abstracted empiricism" from "grand theory" (1959: esp. 124-25).

unnecessary complexity and, according to the rule of parsimony, should be discarded.

It should be emphasized that the decisive comparison argued by the rule of parsimony is between the theory in question and another possible theory, rather than between the theory and the substantive realm in which it seeks explanatory and predictive power. Indeed, when the latter comparison is made, "the argument can sometimes be made *against* a theory . . . that the trouble with it is that it is too simple; Nature sometimes seems to prefer complexity . . . . [and therefore] the progress of science is not always in the direction of the simpler theory" (Kaplan 1964:317-318). But in the former comparison, between theories, "we are to introduce a complicating factor [into the theory of concern] only if we have reason to expect error from its omission" (Kaplan 1964:318). Otherwise, the equally error-free, but simpler, theory is to be preferred.

Thus, for example, Durkheim rejected the theory that suicide could be explained as genetically inherited behavior on the ground that "in families where repeated suicides occur, they are performed almost identically. They take place not only at the same age, but even in the same way. . . . In a case often quoted . . . the same weapon served a whole family at intervals of several years" (1951:97). Durkheim found any theory that would "admit the existence of a [hereditary] tendency to suicide by hanging or shooting" (1951:97) ridiculous. And although he did not give explicit reasons for this opinion, a likely possibility is that such a theory would have to be extremely complex — positing, perhaps, a distinct gene for every conceivable way of committing suicide, another for every conceivable life-space time and place at which it could be committed, and so on and on. To such an impossibly baroque inheritance theory, Durkheim preferred the presumably much simpler social contagion theory.

Popper offers a clear reason for the rule of parsimony in

theory construction: simpler theories are more readily testable.

> To understand [why simplicity is so highly desirable] there is no
> need for us to assume a "principle of economy of thought" or
> anything of the kind. Simple statements . . . are to be prized more
> highly than less simple ones *because they tell us more; because their
> empirical content is greater; because they are better testable . . . .*
> From my point of view, a system must be described as *complex in
> the highest degree* if . . . one holds fast to it as a system established
> forever which one is determined to rescue, whenever it is in danger,
> by the introduction of auxiliary hypotheses. For the degree of fal-
> sifiability of a system thus protected is zero (1961:142, 145).

Language

The usefulness of any given kind of language in formulating
empirical theory depends entirely on the extent to which its
symbols and the rules governing their use (that is, its vocabulary and grammar) correspond to, and can therefore represent,
the empirical observations and generalizations to which the
theory refers. In other words, it is useful for theoretic purposes
to have a language that has a logical structure or that can
express causality only because empirical observations seem to
reflect such types of Necessity, not because logical or causal
structures have particular values in themselves.[33] Mathematical
language, for example, has great theoretic utility only because
its symbols and rules seem to correspond to an extremely wide
range of empirical observations. Specifically, the mathematical
procedures called addition, multiplication, squaring, integrating, etc. — and, of course "numbering" itself — are only useful,

33. Thus, the verification of complex theories via tests of one or more of
their logical implications (see Zetterberg 1963:75-76) depends entirely on the
assumption that "nature is logical." But Bohm's principle of the "qualitative
infinity of nature" (1961:134) implies that nature may also be nonlogical. On
"[mapping] the structure of the language on the structure of the facts," see
Wartofsky (1968: esp. 134-139). For discussion of "reference, abstraction, and
structure," as features of scientific languages, see Wartofsky (1968:124-134).

scientifically, because they correspond to observed empirical processes inhering in such wide-ranging phenomena as homicide, gravitational attraction, interpersonal influence, intergalactic influence, the transmutation of energy and mass, changes in the size of bacterial, insect, and human population, economic supply, demand, and price fluctuations, affect in three-person groups, genetic inheritance, and so on. In fact, new varieties of mathematics have been invented or brought into use (for example, the calculus and tensor mathematics) in response to noncorrespondence between old varieties of mathematics and new empirical observations. Thus, the first scientific question to be asked about a given kind of theoretic language is its "suitability": whether its symbols and rules generally correspond to the observed phenomena and relationships that are the subjects of the theory.

But observations and generalizations themselves depend not only on the "true" nature of empirical reality — on *what* is presumably being observed — but also on the state to which a given science (or scientist) has advanced conceptually and technically — on *how* and *how well* one observes. And these latter, in turn, depend as much on the observer's ideas — his conceptual vocabulary and relational grammar — as on his eyes and other instruments of observation. Thus, not only do empirical observations and generalizations affect selection of the language in which they become symbolized, but the reverse: the language in which theories are formulated affects the hypotheses, empirical observations, generalizations, and tests that can then be made. It follows that a theorist should select a language that is in some sense "better" than the empirical generalizations on which his theory is based, so that the new hypotheses, observations, generalizations, and tests to which the theory gives rise will be "better" than the preceding ones.

But by what criteria can one kind of language be termed "better" than another, for scientific purposes? There are at least four possible criteria. First, the language should quickly and systematically reveal logical inconsistencies and contradictions, whether these fall between hypothesis and observation, between observation and generalization, between generalization and theory, between decisions about hypotheses and theory, within theory itself, or wherever. To do this, the language must be determinate, in the double sense that "the class of things designated by a term is . . . sharply and clearly demarcated from . . . the class of things not so designated," and that "distinctions signified by the terms . . . suffice to characterize more narrowly drawn but important differences between the things denoted by the terms" (Nagel 1961:8). The language, in short, must be capable of making highly explicit, unambiguous statements, since statements that can have several different but equally reasonable interpretations may hide crucial inconsistencies and contradictions behind a suggestive, connotative "richness" that is vital to poetry but mortal to science.[34]

Second, the language should be as universally and as unequivocally understood as possible, so that theories will require only a minimum of translation from one scientific culture or discipline to another, and from one national culture to another. The language should carry as few culture-bound implications as possible, to be free of the ideological prejudices that national cultures so often impose on scientific work, and to guarantee that statements made in the language will be freely communicable within and between scientific disciplines and thus will be maximally open to criticism.

Third, the language should be flexible, in the sense of being as capable of highly specific or highly complex statements as of

34. Durkheim criticized "the words of everyday language" for being "always susceptible of more than one meaning," and he warned that "the scholar employing them in their accepted use without further definition would risk serious misunderstanding. Not only is their meaning so indefinite as to vary, from case to case, with the needs of argument, but . . . categories of very different sorts of fact are indistinctly combined under the same heading, or similar realities are differently named (1951:41)."

general or simple statements, and in the sense of containing precise rules for transforming one into the other.

Finally, the language should encourage extension of the theories that employ it independently of empirical observation and generalization. That is, the language should enable the scientist to manipulate readily the symbols and sentences of the theory as pure abstractions,[35] and thus to draw out their logical implications without reference to actual observations in hand. The empirical validity of such an extension can then be tested through new observations. Hempel cites Euclidean geometry as an example of a theory having this quality:

> Pure geometry does not express any assertions about the spatial properties and relations of objects in the physical world. A physical geometry, i.e., a theory which deals with the spatial aspects of physical phenomena, is obtained from a system of pure geometry by giving the primitives a specific interpretation in physical terms. Thus, e.g., to obtain the physical counterpart of pure Euclidean geometry, points may be interpreted as approximated by small physical objects. . . . This interpretation turns the postulates and theorems of pure geometry into statements of physics, and the question of their factual correctness now permits — and, indeed, requires — empirical tests. . . . If the evidence obtained by suitable methods is unfavorable, the Euclidean form of geometry may well be replaced by some non-Euclidean version which, in combination with the rest of physical theory, is in better accord with observational findings. In fact, just this has occurred in the general theory of relativity (1952:34).

And Braithwaite enumerates further instances of mathematical development independently of scientific observation and theory, and notes some positive consequences:

> It has been a fortunate fact in the modern history of physical science that the scientist constructing a new theoretical system has nearly

35. Braithwaite says, "without thinking of the meanings of the sentences" (1960:23).

always found that the mathematics he required for his system had already been worked out by pure mathematicians for their own amusement. Thus Einstein, in developing general relativity (1915), had Riemann's non-Euclidean geometry (1854) and Ricci's tensor calculus (1887) ready to hand; and the non-commutative multiplication used in quantum mathematics (1925-7) had been worked out in connection with Cagley's matrices (1858) and with operational methods for handling differential equations (Boole, 1844). . . . The moral for statesmen would seem to be that, for proper scientific "planning," pure mathematicians should be endowed fifty years ahead of scientists (1960:48-49).

In all four respects — determinacy, universality, flexibility, and abstractness — the mathematical kind of language seems clearly superior to the verbal kind.[36] As Nagel puts it:

A numerical evaluation of things is only one way of making evaluations of certain selected characters, although it is so far the best. It is pre-eminently the best, because in addition to the obvious advantage they have as a universally recognized language, numbers make possible a refinement of analysis without loss of clarity; and their emotionally neutral character permits a symbolic rendering of invariant relations in a manifold of changing qualities. Mathematics expresses the recognition of a necessity which is not human (1960:-122).

To put this claim in terms of the present essay, one might argue succinctly that mathematical language is clearly superior to verbal in unequivocally delineating, and therefore differentiating, the substantive and spatiotemporal scope and the level of abstraction of theories. Therefore, as Blalock says, eventually we must accomplish the translation of all our verbal theories into mathematical terms:

The careful reworking of verbal theories is undoubtedly one of the

36. A third kind of theoretic language that is intimately related to the mathematical, namely, the graphic, will not be discussed here; see, however, Boulding (1963) and Stinchcombe (1968) for examples.

most challenging tasks confronting us. The major portion of this enterprise will undoubtedly consist of clarifying concepts, eliminating or consolidating variables, translating existing verbal theories into common languages, searching the literature for propositions, and looking for implicit assumptions connecting the major propositions in important theoretical works. The final translation into formal mathematics, and the actual use of mathematical reasoning, would seem to be a relatively simpler task that can be performed by a smaller group of specialists. The more difficult prior task can be accomplished by social scientists without such technical training, provided there is an awareness of both the potentialities and limitations of mathematical formulations of different types (1969:27-28).

Finally, it may be useful to recall that earlier in this book (see Chapter 4), I suggested that a full evaluation of a given theory requires its examination not only for internal structural features representing its logical consistency and freedom from tautology, and not only for external correspondences to observations and empirical generalizations representing its substantive truth-value, but also for certain other features representing its formal informational value. The discussion above has been aimed at specifying four of these features: substantive and spatiotemporal scope, level of abstraction, parsimony, and language. We may conclude that a given theory of a particular class of phenomena is superior to others seeking to explain the same phenomena if it is more logically consistent and freer from tautology; more thoroughly verified by empirical test of deduced hypotheses; if it has higher substantive scope, spatiotemporal scope, level of abstraction, and parsimony in its statements; and if it has highest determinacy, universality, flexibility, and abstractness in its language.

Chapter Seven

Conclusions

It seems worthwhile to recall — and to elaborate somewhat — two of the possible uses of this book that were mentioned in the Preface. There I suggested that, among other things, (1) the book may provide a framework for classifying researches both within a particular scientific field and across all such fields; and (2) it may facilitate constructing and integrating parts within a given research. Let us consider these claims with reference, first, to the general discussion here of Figure 1, and then with reference to the subsequent discussion of theories.

First. The logical structures of a large variety of possible problems,[1] researches, and specializations in a given scientific field may be systematically differentiated according to Figure 1. That is, Figure 1 suggests that such structures may range from an exclusive focus on any one of the informational components, methodological controls, or information transformations (or, indeed, any single aspect of such an element) shown there, to any possible combination of these elements. But by specifying the elements to which this very large variety of problem, re-

1. For discussion of some aspects of *informational* problems and problem-finding in sociology, see Merton (1959: ix-xxxiv), and Greer (1969:8-18). For a discussion of some aspects of *methodological* problems, see Lazarsfeld (1959) and Kaplan (1964:23-29).

search, and specialization structures may be reduced, Figure 1 should be useful in analyzing similarities and differences among them. One can imagine using the elements of Figure 1 to code what might be called the formal (as distinct from substantive) "profile" of an entire field, as interpreted, say, by analysis of the articles published in its journals or papers read at its meetings. One could analyze changes in the profile of a given field, similarities and differences between the profiles of several fields, or of several individual scientists or several "schools" within a single field, etc.

In general, this use of Figure 1 should facilitate answers to a wide variety of questions in the sociology and history of science; for example: Is there an evolutionary pattern with respect to the formal attentions of a field? If so, does this pattern parallel the field's substantive evolution? What are the social structural (for example, recruitment, training, funding, prestige hierarchies, communications networks, etc.) influences on and consequences of the formal profile of a given field? When and why are formally different kinds of "crises," "revolutions," and "serendipitous events" likely to occur?[2] And so on.

Second. Figure 1 should be useful also as a set of guidelines

2. Although Kuhn discusses the revolutionary impact of crises in scientific paradigms as a whole, and although his most explicit definition of a "paradigm" specifies "law, theory, application, and instrumentation" (1964:-10) as its components, he does not discuss this specification further; nor does he examine the causes, developmental sequences, and consequences of different kinds of crises that may originate in different components. Popper, however, provides discussion of at least one kind of crisis. He says that when "the consequences of two theories differ so little in all fields of application that the very small differences between the calculated observable events cannot be detected, owing to the fact that the degree of precision attainable in our measurements is not sufficiently high, [it] will then be impossible to decide by experiment between the two theories, without first improving on technique of measurement (1961:124)." And Kaplan (1964:135) approvingly quotes Jevons: "the invention of an instrument has usually marked, if it has not made, an epoch." Thus, it would appear that some crises are resolved by new instrumentation, as others may be resolved by new theories, or new scaling and measurement techniques, and so forth.

for individual researchers in designing studies. Thus, if one decides to do a study that seeks to develop a particular empirical generalization, Figure 1 indicates the kinds of methodological and informational problems that should be attended to, and it indicates the degree of direct pertinence that should be assigned to each. After defining his substantive area of focus, perhaps the most important research decision a given investigator can make is just this specification of formal aspects of his research problem and of the path to its proposed solution.

Decisions of this kind constitute a guide to the more detailed design of his research, as well as to the basic form of its presentation when it has been completed. For example, the investigator can best formulate hypotheses in a way that will be maximally testable by deliberately anticipating each methodological control and each information transformation that must be accomplished before (and after) the test is made.[3] He can choose or devise appropriate instruments, populations, and samples, scales, and measurement procedures far in advance of actually using them; and, with experience, he can estimate a time schedule for each phase of the research work and for the entire effort. In addition, he can foresee and recognize the moment when the research is completed. (This latter is a practical decision of no small import since, assuming that all things are connected, it is possible, although one may begin with a "small" problem, to follow its ramifications indefinitely, without closure.) But perhaps most important of all, because the general structure of the scientific process as a whole and of its several components and controls is not only relatively unambiguous but universally understood among scientists, the individual investigator can anticipate the criticism of his colleagues. In this way, scientific criticism becomes scientific *self*-criticism as well.

3. For example, Stinchcombe says: "In order to construct theories for a science, we must have in mind the logical requirements for testing the theories against the facts" (1968:15). See also Blalock (1969:8).

The discussion focusing on theories (Chapter 6), that has followed the general explication of Figure 1, may have two uses similar to those just discussed. That is, the discussion may facilitate classifying theories within a given substantive field and across many such fields, and also facilitate constructing and integrating parts and dimensions of a given theory. Thus, one might ask: Does the hierarchical or the concatenated type of theory predominate in different substantive fields, at different times, in the presence of different social structural features? More generally, what empirical relations prevail among all of the principal formal dimensions of theories discussed here (including internal structure, scope, level of abstraction, simplicity, and language), and between them and social structural factors? What are the frequencies with which different explanatory-predictive strategies are chosen in different fields, at different times, and in the presence of different social structural features? How, if at all, are these strategies empirically related to the formal dimensions of theories discussed here? Further, when one is not analyzing several theories, but constructing a particular theory, the formal aspects of theory discussed here may serve as a convenient list of alternatives for conscious choice: Should the theory have a concatenated or hierarchical structure? What should be its scope and level of abstraction? Can it be further simplified? In what language should it be cast?

The above claims regarding the potential usefulness of this essay rest on its explicitly schematic qualities. However, it is now important to temper those qualities with some comments regarding unschematic elements of "creativity," "imagination," "art," and "intuition" in the scientific process.[4] Kaplan offers one clue to the creative elaboration of such an explicitly schematic view as I have presented here, when he distinguishes

4. I am indebted to Diana Crane (private communication) for persuasively arguing against a presentation of the scientific process that makes it out to be extremely regularized and rational, even though I have probably not followed her views fully.

between "the logic-in-use" and "the reconstructed logic" of a science. The first is "what is actually being done by scientists," while the second "idealizes the logic of science . . . in showing us what it *would* be if it were extracted and refined . . . " (1964:10,11). In discussing these two logics, Kaplan suggests one guide to the creative elaboration mentioned above:

> The logic-in-use depends on context to provide sufficient closure for the particular use of the law then and there to be made. In reconstructed logic a formulation becomes fully specified only when we insert an "other things being equal" clause to complete the closure. . . . The uncertainty in the qualifying clause is the price we pay for the formal closure achieved by making the abstraction. . . . When the student first learning the gas laws asks why a gas doesn't completely disappear at a sufficiently low temperature, thus violating the law of conservation of mass . . . it is . . . appropriate to make clear to him the gas laws no longer apply, to the same degree of approximation, in the neighborhood of absolute zero (1964:95-96).

It is thus trained *attention to context*[5] that can provide at least the beginnings of creative application of any scheme — including the one presented here.

Finally, I would stress the point with which this book began: the scientific process is but one way of generating and testing the truth of statements about the world of human experience. The particular statements that the scientific process has vali-

5. Sensitivity to contextual differences (of a public-private kind) seems also responsible for the contrast between the reported formalization of a given study, after the fact, and its actual formalization, when in process. Merton has pointed out that "The record of science will inevitably differ according to whether it is intended to contribute to current scientific knowledge or to an improved historical understanding of how scientific work develops. . . . What must be emphasized here is that this practice of glossing over the actual course of inquiry results largely from the mores of scientific publication which call for a passive idiom and format of reporting which imply that ideas develop without benefit of human brain and that investigations are conducted without benefit of the human hand" (1967:5-6). And Kaplan (1964:53) quotes Dewey as having said, "There is nothing more deceptive than the seeming simplicity of scientific procedure as it is reported in logical treatises."

dated at any given moment may be either more true or less true than the statements validated at that time by other ways; and in any case, whether the science-validated statements are actually true or not, our belief in their truth must remain provisional. As Karl Popper eloquently says:

> The demand for scientific objectivity makes it inevitable that every scientific statement must remain *tentative for ever* . . . . It is not his *possession* of knowledge, or irrefutable truth, that makes the man of science, but his persistent and recklessly critical *quest* for truth (1961:280-281).

And in that quest,

> We do not stumble upon our experiences, nor do we let them flow over us like a stream. Rather, we have to be active: we have to "*make*" our experiences. It is we who always formulate the questions to be put to nature; it is we who try again and again to put these questions so as to elicit a clear-cut "yes" or "no" (for nature does not give an answer unless pressed for it). And in the end, it is again we who give the answer; it is we ourselves who, after severe scrutiny, decide upon the answer which we put to nature . . . (1961:280).

In science (as in "everyday life"), things must be believed to be seen, as well as seen to be believed; and questions must already be answered a little, if they are to be asked at all.

REFERENCES

Asch, Solomon E. "Effects of Group Pressure Upon the Modification and Distortion of Judgments." In *Readings in Social Psychology,* edited by Eleanor E. Maccoby, Theodore M. Newcomb, and Eugene L. Hartley. New York: Holt, 1958:174-183.

Bales, Robert F. *Interaction Process Analysis.* Cambridge, Mass.: Addison-Wesley, 1950.

Barton, Allen H. "The Concept of Property-Space in Social Research." In *The Language of Social Research,* edited by Paul F. Lazarsfeld and Morris Rosenberg. Glencoe, Ill.: The Free Press, 1955:40-53.

Bergmann, Gustav. *Philosophy of Science.* Madison, Wis.: The University of Wisconsin Press, 1957.

Black, Max. "The Justification of Induction." In *Philosophy of Science Today,* edited by Sidney Morgenbesser. New York: Basic Books, 1967:190-200.

Blalock, Hubert M. Jr. and Ann B. Blalock. *Methodology in Social Research.* New York: McGraw-Hill, 1968.

Blalock, Hubert M. Jr. *Theory Construction.* Englewood Cliff, N. J.: Prentice-Hall, 1969.

Bohm, David. Causality and Chance in Modern Physics. London: Routledge and Kegan Paul, 1957. Reprint. New York: First Harper Torchbook Edition, 1961.

Boudon, Raymond. "A New Look at Correlation Analysis." In *Methodology in Social Research,* edited by Hubert M. Blalock, Jr. and

Ann B. Blalock. New York: McGraw-Hill, 1968.

Boulding, Kenneth E. *Conflict and Defense.* New York: Harper & Bros., 1962. Reprint. New York: First Harper Torchbook Edition, 1963.

Braithwaite, Richard Bevan. *Scientific Explanation.* Cambridge: Cambridge University Press, 1953. Reprint. New York: First Harper Torchbook Edition, 1960.

Campbell, Donald T. "Common Fate, Similarity, and Other Indices of the Status of Aggregates of Persons as Social Entities." *Behavioral Science.* vol. 3., 1958:14-25.

Carnap, Rudolf. *Philosophical Foundations of Physics.* New York: Basic Books, 1966.

Costner, Herbert L., and Robert K. Leik. "Deductions from 'Axiomatic Theory' ". *American Sociological Review,* vol. 29, No. 6, Dec., 1964:819-835.

Crane, Diana. *Invisible Colleges and Social Circles: A Sociological Interpretation of Scientific Growth.* Chicago: University of Chicago Press, forthcoming.

Douglas, Jack D. *The Social Meanings of Suicide.* Princeton, N.J.: Princeton University Press, 1967.

Dubin, Robert. *Theory Building.* New York: The Free Press, 1969.

Dumont, Richard G. and William J. Wilson. "Aspects of Concept Formation, Explication, and Theory Construction in Sociology." *American Sociological Review,* vol. 29, No. 6, December, 1967:-985-995.

Duncan, Otis Dudley. "A Socioeconomic Index for All Occupations." In *Occupations and Social Status,* edited by A. J. Reiss, Jr. New York: Free Press, 1961.

————. "Contingencies in Constructing Causal Models." In *Sociological Methodology 1969,* edited by Edgar F. Borgatta. San Francisco: Jossey-Bass, 1969:74-112.

————. "Path Analysis: Sociological Examples." American Journal of Sociology, Vol. 72, July 1966:1-16.

Durkheim, Emile. *Suicide.* New York: Free Press, 1951.

————. *The Rules of Sociological Method.* Chicago: University of Chicago Press, 1938. Reprint. First Free Press Paperback, 1964.

Feigl, Herbert. "Notes on Causality." In *Readings in The Philosophy of Science,* edited by Herbert Feigl and May Brodbeck. New York:

Appleton- Century-Crofts, Inc., 1953:408-418.

Gibbs, Jack P. "Suicide." In *Contemporary Social Problems,* edited by Robert K. Merton and Robert A. Nisbet. 2nd ed. New York: Harcourt, Brace and World, 1966.

Gibbs, Jack P., ed. *Suicide.* New York: Harper and Row, 1968.

Glaser, Barney G. and Anselm L. Strauss. *The Discovery of Grounded Theory.* Chicago: Aldine Publishing Co., 1967.

Greer, Scott. *The Logic of Social Inquiry.* Chicago: Aldine Publishing Co., 1969.

Guttman, Louis. "The Basis for Scalogram Analysis." In *Measurement and Prediction,* edited by Samuel A. Stouffer, et al. Princeton, N.J.: Princeton University Press, 1950.

Hanson, Norwood Russell. "Observation and Interpretation." In *Philosophy of Science Today,* edited by Sidney Morgenbesser. New York: Basic Books, 1967:89-99.

Hatt, Paul K. and C. C. North. "Jobs and Occupations: A Popular Evaluation," *Opinion News,* September, 1947:3-13.

Heise, David R. "Problems in Path Analysis and Causal Inference." In *Sociological Methodology 1969,* edited by Edgar F. Borgatta. San Francisco: Jossey-Bass, 1969:38-73.

Hempel, Carl G. *Aspects of Scientific Explanation.* New York: Free Press, 1965.

————."Methods of Concept Formation in Science." In *International Encyclopedia of Unified Science.* Chicago: University of Chicago Press, 1952.

Homans, George C. *The Human Group.* New York: Harcourt, Brace and World, 1950.

Kaplan, Abraham. *The Conduct of Inquiry.* San Francisco: Chandler Publishing Company, 1964:327-351.

Kuhn, Thomas S. *The Structure of Scientific Revolutions.* Chicago: The University of Chicago Press, 1962. Reprint. First Phoenix Edition, 1964.

Land, Kenneth C. "Principles of Path Analysis." In *Sociological Methodology, 1969,* edited by Edgar F. Borgatta. San Francisco: Jossey-Bass, 1969:3-37.

Lazarsfeld, Paul F., and Morris Rosenberg, eds. *The Language of Social Research.* Glencoe, Ill.: The Free Press, 1955.

Lazarsfeld, Paul F. "Problems in Methodology." In *Sociology Today,* edited by Robert K. Merton, Leonard Broom, and Leonard S. Cottrell, Jr. New York: Basic Books, 1959.

Lazerwitz, Bernard. "Sampling Theory and Procedures." In *Methodology in Social Research,* edited by Hubert M. Blalock, Jr. and Ann B. Blalock. New York: McGraw-Hill, 1968.

Malinowski, Bronislaw. *Magic, Science, and Religion and Other Essays,* Glencoe, Ill.: The Free Press, 1948.

Merton, Robert K. "Notes on Problem-Finding in Sociology." In *Sociology Today,* edited by Robert K. Merton, Leonard Broom, Leonard S. Cottrell, Jr. New York: Basic Books, 1959:ix-xxxiv.

————. *On Theoretical Sociology.* New York: The Free Press, 1967.

————. *Social Theory and Social Structure.* Rev. and enlarged. Glencoe, Ill.: The Free Press, 1957.

Mills, C. Wright. *The Sociological Imagination.* New York: Oxford University Press, 1959.

Montague, William Pepperell. *The Ways of Knowing.* New York: Macmillan, 1925.

Nagel, Ernest. "Measurement." Erkenntis, II Band, Heft 5, 1932. Reprinted in *Philosophy of Science,* edited by Arthur Danto and Sidney Morgenbesser. Cleveland: World Publishing Co., 1960:121-140.

————. "The Nature and Aim of Science." In *Philosophy of Science Today,* edited by Sidney Morgenbesser. New York: Basic Books, 1967:3-13.

————. *The Structure of Science.* New York: Harcourt, Brace and World, Inc., 1961.

Popper, Karl R. *The Logic of Scientific Discovery.* New York: Science Editions, 1961.

Quine, Willard V. "Necessary Truth." In *Philosophy of Science Today,* edited by Sidney Morgenbesser. New York: Basic Books, 1967:46-54.

Scheffler, Israel. "Explanation, Prediction, and Abstraction." *The British Journal for the Philosophy of Science,* Vol. VII, No. 28, 1957. Reprinted in *Philosophy of Science,* edited by Arthur Danto and Sidney Morgenbesser. Cleveland: World Publishing Co., 1960:-274-287.

Sherif, Muzafer. "Group Influences Upon the Formation of Norms and Attitudes." In *Readings in Social Psychology,* edited by Eleanor E. Maccoby, Theodore M. Newcomb, and Eugene L. Hartley. New York: Holt 1958:219-232.

Stevens, S. S. "On the Theory of Scales of Measurement." *Science,* Vol. 103, No. 2684, 1946:677-680.

Stinchcombe, Arthur L. *Constructing Social Theories.* New York: Harcourt, Brace and World, 1968.

Watson, W. H. "On Methods of Representation." From *On Understanding Physics.* Cambridge (England): University Press, 1938. Reprinted in *Philosophy of Science,* edited by Arthur Danto and Sidney Morgenbesser. Cleveland: World Publishing Co., 1960:226-244.

Wartofsky, Marx W. *Conceptual Foundations of Scientific Thought: An Introduction to Philosophy of Science.* New York: Macmillan, 1968.

Webb, Eugene J., Donald T. Campbell, Richard D. Schwartz, and Lee Sechrest. *Unobtrusive Measures.* Chicago: Rand McNally and Co., 1966.

Weber, Max. *From Max Weber: Essays in Sociology.* New York: Oxford University Press, 1946.

—————. *The Theory of Social and Economic Organization.* New York: Free Press, 1947.

Wilson, William J. and Richard G. Dumont. "Rules of Correspondence and Sociological Concepts." *Sociology and Social Research,* Vol. 52, No. 2, January, 1968:217-227.

Zetterberg, Hans L. *On Theory and Verification in Sociology.* Stockholm: Almqvist and Wiksell, 1954.

—————. *On Theory and Verification in Sociology.* Rev. Totowa, N. J.: Bedminster Press, 1963.

—————. *On Theory and Verification in Sociology,* 3rd ed., enlarged. Totowa, N. J.: Bedminster Press, 1966.

Name Index

Asch, Solomon E., 13

Bales, Robert F., 71
Barley, Betsy, 13
Barton, Allen H., 100-101
Bergmann, Gustav, 17, 97, 99
Bergson, Henri, 50
Black, Max, 42
Blalock, Hubert M., Jr., 17, 27,
    56, 65, 79-80, 83, 94,
    96-97, 99, 104-105, 108,
    109, 118-119, 125
Bohm, David, 17, 56, 64, 73, 90,
    92, 102-103, 104, 114
Boudon, Raymond, 101
Boulding, Kenneth E., 118
Braithwaite, Richard Bevan, 33,
    42, 47, 57, 65, 89, 92,
    97-98, 100, 117-118
Bridgman, Percy W., 53

Campbell, Donald T., 83, 105
Carnap, Rudolf, 99
Costner, Herbert L., 65-66, 96-97
Crane, Diana, 22, 126

Darwin, Charles, 13
Douglas, Jack D., 25
Dubin, Robert, 57, 64, 67, 73, 106
Dumont, Richard G., 55
Duncan, Otis Dudley, 72, 101
Durkheim, Emile, 25-29, 83,
    101-102, 105, 113, 116

Einstein, Albert, 50-51, 118

Feigl, Herbert, 64, 92

Galileo, 13
Gibbs, Jack P., 25
Gibbs, Willard, 58
Glaser, Barney G., 22, 95
Greer, Scott, 17, 57, 82, 123
Guttman, Louis, 72

Hanson, Norwood Russell, 34
Hatt, Paul K., 73
Heise, David R., 101
Hempel, Carl G., 53-55, 58-59,
    66, 95-96, 97, 111, 117
Hill, Richard J., 20

Subject Index